Party

Perfect and

Pampered

Also by **SALLY HOLBROOK:**

Sun, Sand and Sausage Pie
... and Beach House Memories

a cookbook

Edited by *Diane Macfarland*
Cover design, illustrations and layout by *Rasa Arbas Chamberlain*
Photography by *Robin M. Banks*
Flowers by *Mary Faulkingham*
Color separation by *B. J. Graphics*
Print production by *John Georgopoulos*

Publisher's Cataloging in Publication

Holbrook, Sally
Party Perfect and Pampered: the
Ultimate Party Book/Sally Holbrook
p.cm.
Includes index
ISBN 0-9631225-1-7

1. Entertaining.   I. Title

TX731.H65 1995   642'.4
                         QB194-21172

Library of Congress Catalog Card Number 94-73987

Copyright © 1995 by Sally Holbrook

Printed in the United States of America
First Edition – First Printing

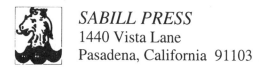

SABILL PRESS
1440 Vista Lane
Pasadena, California 91103

Party
Perfect and
Pampered

... The Ultimate Party Book

By SALLY HOLBROOK

CONTENTS

PHOTOGRAPHS AND ILLUSTRATIONS

This book is lovingly dedicated to my son Bobby

ACKNOWLEDGMENTS

My thanks to my husband, Bill, for his generous and time-consuming help and support. Many of his suggestions have been incorporated into the pages of this book.

Also, my thanks to Nancy Nashu, Mike Boone, David Chaparro, Barbara Gee, Barbara Sargeant, Lucille Maxwell and Susan Bansmer, whose party ideas and suggestions have influenced the development of this book, and some of whose recipes are reflected in the last chapter.

Special thanks to my editor, Diane Macfarland, whose help has been invaluable.

Finally, I wish to express my gratitude to my mother and my mother-in-law, two extremely capable and practiced party givers, for their inspiration.

The recipe for **Irish Stew** appearing on page 169 is reprinted from *Cooking for Holidays and Celebrations* by Marlene Sorosky with permission of The Putnam Publishing Group. Copyright © 1994 by Marlene Sorosky.

The recipe for **Mauna Lau Dressing** appearing on page 177 is reprinted from *Hawaiian Cookbook* by Roana and Gene Schindler with permission of Dover Publications. Copyright © 1970 by Roana and Gene Schindler.

The recipe for **Orange Fantasia** appearing on page 185 is reprinted from *Bon Appétit* with permission of The Condé Nast Publications, Inc. *Bon Appétit* is a registered trademark of Advance Magazine Publications Inc. and is published through its division The Condé Nast Publications, Inc. Copyright © 1995 by The Condé Nast Publications, Inc.

PROLOGUE

This book is intended to be a **guide** for novice party givers, and to provide a potpourri of new ideas and reminders for the more experienced hostess.

By sharing my experiences and suggestions, I hope to help those of you who are beginners to overcome normal hesitancies, assist in developing your natural creativity and help you build confidence in your own party giving skills.

But this is **not** a book solely for women. Men also give parties – and they, too, will benefit from my suggestions.

Do not feel that you must be fancy or fanciful with the themes, decorations or favors I have suggested in order to have a fun, wonderful and beautiful party.

A good party is made up of many elements – and people are the most important. The rest you can simplify or embellish, depending upon your budget, your timetable, your taste and your preferences. Set the stage "As You Like It."

My wish is to help make party giving easy and great fun for you, and to help you obtain your party giving goals with total confidence.

Start your own traditions. Pick a single party theme (a special occasion, your favorite holiday or time of year, for example) for an annual party. Take your time planning and organizing the event so you can enjoy every step along the way.

Later, after you have developed a feel for it, you may wish to add additional parties or gatherings to your list.

There are many places in this book where I have intentionally repeated ideas or suggestions because, very often, an idea for one party applies equally well to another type of party.

You will find many instances where I have mentioned specific brand names and the names of certain stores, books, magazines and catalogs. I have done this because I use them and feel comfortable with them; there is no commercial reason whatever for my doing so.

Although I feel comfortable with the companies mentioned and recommend them accordingly, I would encourage you to use the products and services of companies with which you have had satisfactory experiences and with which *you* feel comfortable.

GETTING STARTED

A gathering of just a few friends or family members is reason enough to have a party.

People love to be together with good friends and family, as well as interesting "others," to celebrate a special occasion or just have a good time. Theme or no theme, holiday or any day, whether the menu is filet mignon or a dressed up hot dog, it doesn't matter.

Home is where you can establish your own traditions and where special memories are born. Although we all are inspired and influenced by different people and events, find your own unique style of hostessing – and don't be intimidated by someone else's way of doing things.

Do you prefer country or colonial, contemporary or traditional, plain, fancy or zany, or a combination of any of these? What kind of budget do you have to work with? Are you naturally creative? Do you need suggestions for favors, floral arrangements, menus? As a young married couple, my husband and I lived on a tight budget and I had to learn to entertain on a shoestring. I subscribed to a few magazines and purchased others as they caught my eye in the market or in bookstores. I read every page with relish and cut out recipes and party ideas as I went along, adapting them to my own ideas.

I suggest that you do the same; subscribe to a few magazines to see which ones best fit your personal style and taste. I know I put myself into a glorious mood for entertaining after finishing a relaxing hour or so pouring through magazines such as *Victoria, House Beautiful, Southern Accents, Sunset, Bon Appétit, Better Homes and Gardens, and Gourmet.*

You, too, will probably look forward to each new issue every month; it's a very worthwhile pleasure even if you only get one idea from the whole lot of them.

Cut out pictures and recipes from the magazines when you are through with them and put them into folders, envelopes or boxes and mark them by subject matter. These will be your personal party "collections!"

Keep them nearby so you can refer to them for menus, decorations, themes, favors, flowers, color schemes, etc. Over a period of time you will build quite a file, so it is helpful to go through it about once a year and weed out whatever is no longer of interest. You and your guests will reap the benefits of these efforts.

Try not to be overwhelmed by the material you will read. Enjoy the beauty of the whole picture, and pick out what pleases you, whether it be an arrangement of furniture or flowers, a table setting, a color combination, or a delicious sounding recipe that fits your culinary abilities.

You will find ideas galore wherever you look. You are surrounded by them in stores, someone else's home, out shopping or sightseeing, or on a trip around town. Jot down comments to add to your file; it will soon become a pleasant habit.

Look for ideas for favors, party themes and holiday entertaining. The thought and effort you put into planning the details of your party will demonstrate to your guests how much you appreciate them, and how much you care about them.

Party favors do not have to be purchased. You can have a lot of fun handcrafting things, and it is much easier on the budget. Or you can offer your guests something from your kitchen as a favor, such as homemade candy, cookies, or small loaves of bread.

Even if you are able to spend whatever your heart desires, don't turn over *everything* for someone else to do. Put your own personal imprint on your entertaining. If you let someone else do it all for you, you will have missed out on something special.

If you allow things to get too complicated or too fussy, or if you let yourself take on too many tasks at once, you can become exhausted and overanxious. That may lead you to decide early on that entertaining is not for you, which would be a shame.

I would suggest you start on a small scale. Invite a few good friends, people you feel comfortable with; a group of four to six is about right until you gain confidence. Do not try to be brave and experiment with new and untried recipes unless you know your guests very well, and you are sure it won't bother them, *or you*, if you aren't the early success you had hoped to be.

It is perfectly normal for a host or hostess to experience "party jitters" once in a while. I can't emphasize enough that even the *best cooks* and *chefs* in the world have their failures!

There will be times when things won't work out the way you had planned. Some very talented cooks I know become very nervous and unsure of themselves when they are entertaining another outstanding cook.

So, until you feel confident and comfortable, keep it simple. Even some of the finest chefs will choose pasta, pizza or hamburgers as their favorite off duty foods (a chef and *restaurateur* friend of mine came

for a barbecue dinner one night and said he had forgotten how good a simple steak and baked potato dinner could be).

Always remember that even if your menu is an informal one, **you need to be organized and must plan ahead.** You should prepare food and favors in advance to save yourself from last minute "butterflies." You may have unexpected interruptions, especially if you have small children in the house. If you have not allowed time for problems which might occur, you will be very unhappy and the fun of preparing for the party will be lost.

If you do have children, try to plan your work around their nap time or school time. The older ones can really be quite helpful, and more often than not, they are eager to take part in your party planning and preparing.

As I stated in the prologue, **this book is for men too!** There are many men (married and single) who love to cook, and in fact, some who prefer to take over the culinary tasks entirely. Perhaps both a husband and wife like to cook, and for example, one may have expertise in baking and dessert making and the other with salads and meats. What a great entertaining team two cooks will make!

Bachelors and single fathers often are quite gracious and innovative party hosts. So, wherever I use the word "hostess" throughout these pages, *please* consider it to include "host" as well.

And ladies, don't overlook the variety of talents which your husband might have. Some men are imaginative when it comes to table setting and decorations, and others in food preparation. They will often have an eye for color which will wow us all, and they can be helpful in setting things up and doing the heavy work. So be sure to ask them for suggestions and help regarding all aspects of the party preparations. Make them feel that they are an important participant since, after all, they probably will be the host for most of your parties.

Before your guests arrive, you need to have some time to relax and pamper yourself. Take a nap or a leisurely bath. Later, when the party is over and you have thoroughly spoiled your guests, it's clean up time; but you won't mind because you will be celebrating the success of your party. Turn on the stereo, pour yourself a cool glass of wine or a steaming cup of hot coffee and get to work. After the dishes have been rinsed and stacked or put in the dishwasher, put your feet up, relax, and congratulate yourself on a job well done!

In this book I will share with you parties I have given and parties I have attended. I will suggest ideas for others. I hope you will take these ideas and use them as a guide to help you develop your own style and personal touch. The more you do it, the more creative you will become.

Certain suggestions that I make may be obvious, but they are simply reminders or helpful hints to keep you on the right track. Make this book your "entertainment bible." You might want to take notes or highlight sections for your own personal use.

This book is my way of sharing with you the things I love to do. When you create the perfect party, you should not only pamper your guests but you should also pamper yourself as well – and I will show you how to do it. Now, enjoy and let your imagination run free.

You don't have to just dream of the perfect party, you can make it happen!

PLANNING AND ORGANIZING A PARTY

Be organized – plan and prepare ahead!

The most important ingredient for assuring that your party is a success is planning ahead. I really cannot emphasize this enough.

Your guests are your friends, and you want to make them feel at home. To do that, you need to provide relaxed and pretty surroundings which reflect the mood or theme you have selected for your party. This requires thoughtful planning and organizing well in advance of the event.

With your new confidence will come the relaxed attitude and feeling which will allow you to pamper yourself while you are pampering your guests.

Webster's describes pretty as "pleasing by delicacy or grace, neat or elegant, engaging, good, fine." The thesaurus tells us that synonyms of pretty are "attractive, beautiful, cute, charming, good looking, lovely, graceful."

Nowhere in these definitions is it inferred that *you* must personally create the setting or the food to be served. It doesn't matter if all the menu items are purchased from the deli, the flowers arranged by a florist, or the place cards purchased from your local Hallmark's. However, if you confidently exude your own personal warmth and caring, your party will surely succeed in achieving many of the adjectives listed above.

Do not be intimidated by someone else's style or expertise. We all add our own personal touch to anything we do, from the simplest thing to the most elaborate. *Just relax and do it your way – if you feel good about it, so will your guests.*

Your enthusiasm will become a part of their good time. And don't be afraid to combine the old and traditional with the new and contemporary when you are considering menu items, serving dishes, decorations, favors or flower arrangements.

We must all find our own cooking and decorating style, which will be dependent, in part, on many variables: time (do you work, do you have small children); income (do you have a large, small or nonexistent entertaining budget); your own personal likes and dislikes (do you like informal or formal dinners, barbecues, large or small gatherings); how and where you live (in the city or country, at the seaside or on a lake, in a detached home, condo or apartment).

Remember, everyone is flattered by a little extra attention, which in entertaining, might be as simple as a particularly beautiful decoration or an unusually served meal. For example, picture a pizza sliced and served on a bed of crunchy lettuce in a flat, round basket lined with colorful fabric.

Check List

Make a list of all of the elements of your party to make certain that no detail, no matter how small, has not been forgotten. Have a basic check list which you follow for each occasion. Such a list might include:

- the DATE of your party – be sure it does not conflict with plans your guests have already made for that date

- the KIND of party it is going to be

- your GUEST list – are all guests compatible

- what FAVORS you want to have

- do you want or need PLACE CARDS

- what FLOWERS, decorations and accessories you want

- what is your MENU – check your list of guests' likes and dislikes, and foods to which they are allergic

Keep your notes together: on a clipboard, in a box, or in a folder. Once you have finally organized and expanded the above check list you will be ready to:

- extend INVITATIONS by mail or by telephone

- make a list of COOKING ingredients you will need from the recipes you have chosen

- Save DAYS to shop and cook

- PREPARE those foods which can be made ahead and frozen (appetizers, casseroles, sauces, rolls, some desserts)

- buy or make your FAVORS and/or PLACE CARDS (do this well in advance in case you have interruptions that will delay you)

- if you are having FLOWERS, decide the kind and variety, where they will be put around the house, what containers you will need

- if you plan to have ENTERTAINMENT, decide what that will be: music, parlor games, indoors or outside

- for your own use, make a SEATING chart for a guest list of six or more

- make and store extra bags of ICE in the freezer

Invitations

I like to send the invitations out a month ahead. Hopefully that way everyone will be free to come and will reply promptly. Not everyone is considerate, however, and you may have to call some the week of the party.

In one corner of the invitation, put your phone number beneath or next to the "RSVP;" in the other corner, put the date by which you wish to receive a reply. Also, indicate on the invitation the kind of party that it is going to be and the appropriate dress (casual, costume, informal, formal).

Music

A pretty view or background is always enhanced by music. As long as there are not too many people creating excessive noise, music is a nice way of making guests feel relaxed and welcome.

Aside from hiring professional musicians, you can provide your own sound from your stereos, radios, CD players and tape decks. You can also use your Walkman, concealing it in a secret place such as under the furniture or behind doors or plants. You could borrow others to place in various rooms of the house or yard.

Select your music according to your party theme, choosing favorites from jazz, rock, romantic, country, classical, or even a mixture of appropriate selections. You can purchase tapes or prerecord your selections on blank tapes.

Toasts

Traditionally, toasts are made at various celebrations: birthdays, retirements, weddings and anniversaries; when making a toast, it is customary to raise one's glass in tribute to the honored guest or guests.

Try something a little different: if the toast is for one or more of the guests, place a lighted candle in the center of each guest's dessert, and starting with the host, ask each person to make a wish for the honoree(s) and then blow out his or her own candle. You might write or type various wishes on small pieces of paper which you can then give to each guest as they arrive or attach to their place cards.

You needn't make the wishes too lengthy or complicated; greeting cards are an excellent source of ideas for appropriate sayings. The following are a few suggestions that may be combined or used separately:

- success and prosperity

- beauty and love

- a happy heart

- rainbows and good fortune

- contentment and fulfillment

- marriage and family

- optimism and confidence

- wisdom and courage

- sustaining days and special moments

- inner peace and smiles

- rainbows on rainy days

- health and gratitude

- everything you wish for

- joy and strength on down days

- a wealth of friends to enrich your life

Games

Charades is one of the most popular games for any age group, and is a real icebreaker. It is versatile because categories (names of people, books, music, movies, places, animals) which can easily be acted out by two teams may be chosen to match any party theme.

With guidelines established beforehand, the respective teams draw subjects by lot, which one member then describes in pantomime to his team for it to identify. The main rule is that there be no talking – you must act out the name of the book, play, etc., using signs such as touching your ear to indicate "sounds like."

Gather your team together and pick the words to be acted out. Write them on small pieces of paper and put them in a bowl to be drawn by the opposite team. Begin your pantomime by indicating to your team the category of the name you have drawn by using prearranged signs for book (open hands), song (mouth wide open), movie (one hand shielding the eyes while the other makes a cranking motion), etc. For a western theme party, the categories might include Roy Rogers's horse Trigger (name), "*Home on the Range*" (song), prairie dog (animal), "*High Noon*" (movie).

Another party pleaser is the "potato dance." For this you need a clear space on carpet, bare floor or patio, a medium size potato for each couple, and music. The contestants need not know how to dance or even know their partner – all they must do is move to the beat of the music while keeping the potato between their foreheads.

When the potato falls to the floor, that couple is eliminated. What's fun is the outrageous positions people end up in trying to prevent the potato from slipping down, which it inevitably does, thus eliminating couples one by one until only the winning couple is left.

Another popular and easy icebreaker is to pin the name of a well known personality, whether dead or alive, to the back of each guest as he or she arrives. By questioning each other, with only yes or no answers permitted, each guest must try to guess the name that he or she has been given. The first to do so correctly wins. Don't make the names too easy, and try to search out those which fit the look or personality of the guest.

Books of games can be found at bookstores or libraries.

Suppliers and Professional Services

Learn to use the Yellow Pages to assist you in locating services for party planning: entertainment, serving supplies, equipment rentals, caterers and florists (many will rent small trees, shrubs and flower containers). Borrow needed items from willing friends and family, such as dishes, cooking and serving utensils, needed accessories, plants and flowers. For future reference, keep a record of the suppliers you locate and note the type of party items they supplied, their price lists, and whether they were a good and reliable source.

If your budget will allow, hire someone to help serve and clean up or even cook the meal for you. If you are planning a large gathering, it would be a good idea to hire a bartender, although it can be more personal and relaxing to have the guests help themselves. Your local liquor store can supply you with names of bartenders in the area, or ask your friends who they would recommend.

Many high schools and colleges have employment departments where students eager to earn some extra money can sign up for various jobs. Also, ask your own older children; they might be receptive to an opportunity to earn extra money by helping.

If you are going to have professional help, be sure to call them well in advance. When they arrive, have a list ready for them which includes the following: what you are serving, what cooking (if any) they will have to do, the cooking times for each dish, and what time you want the meal served.

To make certain that specific serving pieces are used as desired for each menu item, write on a slip of paper the food to be served and place it in the appropriate dish. Even if you are doing this work yourself, these helpful "cues" will make any last minute rush much easier for you.

Setting the Table

For a large party, plan to set your tables or buffet a day or two in advance. To avoid dust, cover the dishes and glasses with dish towels. You will need tablecloths or place mats, napkins, silverware, salt and pepper services, glasses (for wine and for water) and one or more centerpieces.

If you are having a buffet, you can tuck the silverware into a napkin – roll it up or make an envelope. Be sure your silver is polished!

If your party is a stand-up, help-yourself, sit-where-you-want cocktail or buffet party, you will need enough room for serving the dinner as well as space to set up a bar (if you are using one). On the other hand, if you are planning a more organized sit-down affair, you will have to allow for both serving and dining tables.

For comfort and intimacy, serve dinner in the dining room buffet-style, or if very informal, serve from the kitchen. This is especially popular with open kitchens. Or you may choose to serve individual plates in the kitchen and have them at each place before the guests are seated.

Personally, I prefer to have each guest serve him or herself – whether it be from an attractively arranged buffet table in the dining room or from pots and pans on the kitchen counter.

How you set up your dining tables depends on the size and shape of the area in which you are entertaining. For most parties, round tables are "friendlier" than rectangular ones, as they tend to make conversation easier.

With a large group of people, and lacking space in your dining room, set up tables in a bedroom or den. Be sure that you have provided a separate area for coats and sweaters, and easy access to the bathroom for all guests.

At times you can end up with more people than you have originally invited or planned on. Invited guests may tell you that they will drop by just for a drink, and then end up staying for dinner. Put extra place mats, silver, napkins and favors where you can get them quickly. You might even have to relinquish your own favor.

Prepare extra food for such contingencies (the leftovers, if any, can be frozen to augment a family meal on another day). Late additions are most difficult when you have planned a sit-down dinner, as you may have to rearrange the seating at the last minute. It does happen, though, so be prepared!

Seating

To plan your seating arrangement, draw circles or rectangles depicting your table shapes on a large piece of paper. Write in the names of your guests in pencil so you can erase and rearrange the names until you are satisfied with the final arrangement.

One of the hardest jobs for a host or hostess is deciding who is to sit next to whom at a sit-down dinner. If you know your friends well, you will know the combinations of people which work the best. For example, place talkative ones next to the quieter ones, or put people with similar interests together. If you have couples who don't like to be separated, put them side by side or across from one another.

You want everyone to feel comfortable and enjoy themselves. If the conversation lags at your table, suggest a topic (not too controversial) such as something you have read in the morning newspaper, in a recent magazine, or something of common interest. If you have more than one table, seat the host and hostess at different tables so each can stimulate the conversation at his or her table. Alternatively, you might ask a trusted friend to perform this function.

Serving Table or Sideboard

If you don't have a suitable serving table or sideboard, bring in a table from some other room or set up a card table or tables. Putting two card tables together avoids crowding the serving dishes. Throw a cloth over the two table tops to make them look like one. If your budget allows (and you have the storage space) purchase two card tables which would be immediately available for expanding the buffet or seating areas.

Folding table tops, which will convert a standard card table into a table for six to eight people, are available at linen supply stores, department stores and are advertised in some catalogs.

Trips to local "flea" markets, garage sales and used or unpainted furniture stores might produce additional sources for appropriate tables and chests. They can be painted, lacquered, stained or simply draped with fabric, tablecloths or colorful sheeting. If all else fails, borrow or consult the Yellow Pages and rent whatever you need.

Serving Pieces

You don't need to have fancy or expensive serving pieces – a plain Pyrex serving dish can be quite attractive when surrounded with a colorful fabric and supported by heavy duty foil. Place your selected fabric (a large dish towel or napkin) on a similarly sized sheet of heavy duty aluminum foil, and mold it to the shape of the serving dish you will use, making a thick ridge along the top of the sides.

Later, when you are ready to serve, press the foil snugly against the sides of the serving dish and allow the fabric to drape over the sides covering the foil. Fold any excess fabric underneath. In picking fabric, follow your chosen color scheme for the occasion or season (flowers, holly, pumpkins, shamrocks, hearts, etc.).

Line terra cotta flowerpots with foil and use them for baking bread or chicken pies, or fill them with ice cream for desserts; fill pumpkins with stews or soups. Check your cupboards for those forgotten jars, dishes or pretty glasses. In the bathroom you might have a pretty canister filled with Q-Tips or cotton balls which you could "borrow" for jelly, honey or mustard. A beautiful crystal pitcher or a silver baby cup make pretty containers for small floral arrangements.

Plates, glassware and flatware may be mixed or matched depending on what you have on hand and the look you want to achieve – whatever makes you feel good.

If you are having an informal party and decide to use paper goods, please make them colorful; if you use white paper plates, "marry" them with brightly colored solid or print napkins. Use heavy duty plates, the large ones for dinner, the small ones for dessert. Plan on one or two dinner size napkins, depending on the menu, and several cocktail napkins per person.

Check the Yellow Pages under "Party Supplies" for rentals. Ask the providers to mail you their brochures so you can check prices and available party supplies.

Dressing up Containers

If glasses (including jelly glasses and Mason-type jars), vases and votives are too plain, wrap them in raffia, ribbon or a colorful fabric. Cover them with sticky floral tape, attach leaves (such as ivy) and flowers, and secure them with raffia or ribbon. Examples of decorated and decorative glassware are pictured on page 93.

Any glass jar can be dressed up with paint, stick-ons or ribbon. For a novel effect, make a "jar hat" – remove the lid from a small jar, which then becomes the base for the jar, and then cut out and form a hat using construction paper for the jar top. A templet (pattern) for making the Easter bunny jar hat cutouts is provided on page 67; the completed Easter bunny jar hat is illustrated in the photograph on page 98. The templet can be used to make hats for any occasion; the ears and whiskers can be omitted as pictured on page 97.

Once decorated, fill these jars with candy or nuts. Decorated jars without lids or hats can become vases to show your prettiest flowers.

Paint designs on terra cotta pots either freehand or using stencils, or spray paint the pots first and then decorate them. Flower pots and vases make wonderful food containers as pictured on page 90.

Dishes and receptacles are no longer just single purpose items. For instance, glasses may become vases; tall vases might hold breadsticks; and decorative ashtrays could be used as butter dishes. Some examples are pictured on page 93.

Be imaginative, perhaps even a little daring. Experiment with a variety of containers (boxes, dishes, jars, pitchers, vases) and all kinds of materials (glass, including Pyrex, wood, pottery, china, leather, basketware) which will hold food, whether hot or cold, wet or dry. For example, at a western or outdoor party, serve your guests water or wine in Mason-type jars.

For lidded jars, try gluing a plain cabinet knob (found at the hardware store) to the top for a different look. The same can be done with cans (like peanut cans) which have plastic lids.

Cloths, Place Mats and Napkins

You will need a 90 inch tablecloth to adequately cover card table "extenders." They can be found in department stores and linen supply stores in multi or solid colors, as well as in patterns.

For added charm, lay a small, contrasting cloth over the top of another one. A lovely antique white or ecru lace cloth, or a beautiful large scarf makes a lovely addition to a plain cloth.

Cloths, place mats and napkins may be purchased in a variety of colors, fabrics and textures – or purchase the fabric and make them yourself. Choose from an exciting array of stripes, plaids, prints, florals, solids or whimsical designs. If you feel comfortable mixing patterns, try teaming florals with stripes or plaids.

Maybe you have a willing friend or wonderful seamstress who will help you; otherwise, if sewing is not your forte, cut the cloths and napkins with pinking scissors and you will have a very acceptable look. Kitchen towels make excellent, though informal, napkins.

The occasion and theme of your party will dictate color and pattern. Annual celebrations are the easy ones: Halloween, Thanksgiving, Christmas, Saint Patrick's Day, Fourth of July, etc. Select ethnic party colors using those from each country's flag. Check store displays and magazine articles, or go to the library to gather information on the national colors appropriate for your ethnic party.

If you have a fussy floral wallpaper in your dining room or a gallery of artwork on the walls, be careful not to get too busy with your table covers, as you would not want them to clash with the special aura of the room.

When you are entertaining outside, picnic-style, the ground may be your dinner table. Checkered tablecloths and colorful sheets are wonderful to use in this case. For variety, try rugs, quilts and beach towels. All of these may also be used to make interesting table covers.

Napkin Rings

I love napkin rings!

A multitude of different types and styles may be found in stores, or you might even make your own. The type and theme of your party will dictate the color and design of the napkin rings.

Try tying the napkins with raffia or ribbon – or use your garden as a source and encircle the napkins with ivy wreaths, slipping a flower (or a bunch of little flowers) underneath. Dry twigs, if they are soft and pliable, can be used in their natural state or sprayed any color you desire (including silver and gold), then wrapped around the napkins. Add leaves, acorns, thistles, tiny succulents or flowers.

If you do use your garden as a source for napkin ring material, do so as late as possible so the flowers don't wilt. Cut the flowers, fit them into the wreaths, then refrigerate them until just before your guests arrive.

For kitchen showers, use cookie cutters as napkin rings.

When I was first married and on a very tight budget, I cut rings from heavy, stiff cardboard wrapping paper tubes and covered them inside and out with fabric, then embellished them with thin ribbon and lace. I painted others or covered them with wrapping paper or wallpaper (doll house wallpaper is excellent for this as the patterns are smaller).

Using your own creative talents, decorate the rings with miniature figures or scenes, flowers, birds or bows. Look for ideas as well as supplies in floral supply stores and miniature stores. You might discover beads, buttons, sequins, lace or rickrack in your sewing box which would make good decorations. Encourage your guests to take their napkin rings home – at Christmas they can be slipped over a tree branch as an ornament and will be a warm reminder of your hospitality.

The photograph on page 83 illustrates several styles of unique and handcrafted napkin rings.

Centerpieces

I believe it is important to put a lot of thought into eye-pleasing centerpieces. Your guests will be looking at them throughout the entire meal, and you want them to contribute toward making everything more enjoyable.

Be sure to keep centerpieces low so people can see the diners across the table. Or, for a more formal affair, you might place the centerpieces on pedestals high enough so people can be seen across the table underneath them.

Arrange your flowers in pots, baskets, glass or silver containers; they can be traditional or contemporary. For teas, you might select teapots, sugar bowls, creamers or cups and saucers to hold flowers.

If you plan to use a silver bowl or a treasured antique, be sure you line the inside with a piece of heavy plastic, or place a small bowl inside, to keep the water (or dirt if you use small plants) from seeping through and possibly damaging the container. After inserting the plastic, trim the excess at the lip of the bowl.

Take a leisurely walk around the house and look for objects in each room which might enhance your table settings or make interesting decorations. A thimble from your sewing box can hold a tiny bouquet of delicate flowers; your husband's humidor or your child's doll dishes (if they will part with them for a few days) make excellent containers for foods and flowers.

Raid your cupboards. You might find some hidden treasures, whether dime store variety or prized antiques, which will add that unusual look you want to achieve. Fill soup bowls, tea cups, egg cups, small brandy snifters, baby cups and silver porringers with miniature flowers. Even laboratory beakers make interesting vases for long-stemmed flowers.

If you plan to use cut flowers, purchase some oasis (a sponge-like block for supporting cut flowers) from your local florist or florist supply store, and thoroughly soak it in water before starting your arrangement. Or "frogs" can be used, but if you don't have the right size you might make a grid at the top of your vase with florist tape, and arrange the flowers so the stems are supported by the grid.

If you have houseplants around, you might use them for your centerpieces by adding cut flowers inserted into little vials of water (found at your local florist) tucked around the plants.

Trailing plants, such as ivy, are especially attractive when used with cut flowers. As an additional enhancement, try placing individual miniature bouquets or nosegays as favors at each guest's place..

The colors and varieties of flowers you use will be dictated by the colors of your dining or serving room, the colors and patterns of your dinnerware and the type and theme of your party. You don't need a course in flower arranging – pick what pleases you and experiment with it. If the arrangement doesn't look right, move the flowers or greens around, placing the taller flowers toward the center.

Mix orange and yellow with red; pink and purple with a touch of red; blue and white with yellow; burgundy or green with gold; pink and blue with yellow. Mother Nature does!

An all white mixture of roses, tulips and Queen Anne's lace is lovely for a bridal or wedding anniversary party. For a soft, ethereal look, combine yellow and pink Peruvian lilies with blue miniature daisies, then add a hint of baby's-breath. I prefer Queen Anne's lace to baby's-breath, but it is not always available.

Roses always seem romantically Victorian to me. Daisies of all kinds and colors can have either a traditional or a contemporary look depending on the type of container you use. Lilies and some agapanthus make stunning tall arrangements. A large shallow bowl of curly succulents with a few agapanthus exploding from the center is more contemporary and quite dramatic.

For a touch of whimsy, use sticky floral tape to attach stalks of asparagus to a plain, straight-sided vase or drinking glass, tie with ribbon or raffia, and fill with daisies – wonderful for a spring brunch or luncheon. Or try a collection of bottles, from small decanters to tiny decorative perfume bottles, filling each with blossoms or buds and grouping them casually down the center of your table or at each guest's place.

Sprays and boughs of evergreens from your garden, or from the florist, make a low and stunning centerpiece for any table, especially during the Christmas holidays. Dress them up with nuts, pine cones, miniature vegetables or an array of fruits (red and green grapes, pomegranates, cranberries, lemons and limes, crab apples) or flowers.

If some of your table greens begin to dry out and fade, spraypaint them gold – pine cones are also attractive when a touch of gold has been added.

For picnics on the lawn or a sandy beach, place sturdy baskets or pots in the center of a large "tablecloth" (which could be a rug, a beach towel, a quilt, etc.) or at the side or corner of a smaller one.

When I have a party in someone's honor, I put one of the flower arrangements in a florist's liner and then in my container. This allows me to give the flowers to the honored guest in a container she can take home with her.

Instead of a floral arrangement, a beautiful piece of porcelain (bird, statue, tureen) makes a unique centerpiece. A tiered bowl of fruit makes an attractive conversation piece as well.

Enhance your arrangements with candlelight – votives, candlesticks and candelabra! Mirrored glass bases can be purchased, and they will dramatically reflect the light.

Place Cards

A place card, or place card/favor, is a necessity for groups of eight or more, certainly for ten and up. You may, of course, forego place cards and write your seating arrangements on a piece of paper, and just before dinner is served, tell each guest personally where he or she is to sit. However, this can become burdensome and delay the start of things, particularly if your presence is needed in the kitchen just at that time.

Listed below are a number of suggestions and ideas for making your own place cards. I encourage you to use your imagination and develop your own unique ideas. You might prefer, however, to purchase them at a stationery store.

- Cut colored construction paper in the desired shape (round, square, heart, turkey, tree, etc.) using regular or pinking scissors. Fill in the guest's name leaving the cards plain, or decorate them using paint, beads, stickers, glitter, dried or fresh flowers, etc. Stand them up at the place settings or tie them to a favor with a thin ribbon.

- On the outside of a folded place card write the guest's name, and on the inside you might write a message or personal note, or copy a short poem or a saying from a greeting card. This is a particularly useful idea when you want to toast an honored guest.

- Write guests' names in the center of small lace paper doilies and glue them to stiff paper; or fold small doilies in half and attach them to a favor with thin ribbon; or attach them to green garden sticks which may later be slipped into a small plant. Centers made of colored fabric or paper can be glued to small doilies, giving them the look of a flower; tie the napkin with a ribbon and attach the little "flower."

- Set regular greeting cards of any size against a glass or rest them on a napkin. Write the guests' names in the upper right hand corner of the envelope where the stamp normally goes (so the guest may reuse the card later if they wish).

- For Halloween, use dime store masks and write the guests' names on the masks with a gold or silver pen. Check with your local art or stationery store for the type of pen which will work best on the mask material. You might also decorate the masks with sequins and feathers.

- Write the names of guests on their wine glasses using craft, or other washable markers, and tie a ribbon around the bases.

- Make a "flag" using a peel-off label and a toothpick. Cut the label to twice the size desired for the flag, remove the backing and fold it in half over the end of the toothpick. Dye the toothpick using food coloring. Labels come in white or various colors and can be decorated with colored ink pens or stick-on designs. After writing the guests' names on the flags, slip the toothpicks into a ribbon or raffia-tied napkin or a tiny potted plant. If you have made miniature loaves of bread for your guests to take home, stick the flags into the top of each loaf.

- For Thanksgiving, spray large leaves gold or silver, or use the beautiful fall leaves just as they are. Write the guests' names on the leaves in gold, silver or black ink.

Favors and Favor/Place Cards

Take time out to look for, or make, the perfect favors for your party. Once you are into it, you will realize how much fun it is. The purpose of the favor is to thank your guests for coming to your party and to show them that you care about them.

Most of the following suggestions for favors need only a simple small card attached with each guest's name on it to make them favor/place cards; others just need the guest's name written directly on the favor itself.

- Fill boxes and baskets of all sizes, colors, shapes and materials with candy and cookies, homemade or bought, or fill them with tiny surprises such as miniature games, Christmas ornaments, etc. Save gift and candy boxes; they can be covered with paper or fabric, or painted and decorated. The photograph on page 97 illustrates several decorated Shaker-type and cardboard boxes ready to be used as favors or favor/place cards.

- Small jars of jams and jellies, or other appropriate foodstuffs tied with a bow, make nice gifts for bridal showers. Set the tiny jars into small baskets for a nice perky touch.

- Paste drawer knobs (pulls) onto the top of lids to give them an added attraction. Wooden knobs can be spray painted or left natural. Hardware stores generally have a wide selection of sizes and shapes from which to choose. These decorated jar and can lids, along with the novel "jar hats," are pictured on page 97.

- Send guests home with small loaves of bread, cookies or candy favors that you have made. Top them with nuts, candy flowers or icing. Christmas flowers may be created using candied cherries for the petals and citron for the leaves. Offer your guests breads in their original baking pans; wrap the pans in fabric and tie with a bow; or place them in baskets, tins or colorful paper tote bags.

- A jumbo cookie with the guest's name on it (use icing tubes from the market) is a delicious bit of whimsy.

- If you have a discount store nearby, you can have a wonderful time shopping not only for boxes and baskets, but for small white porcelain pitchers, lotus bowls, ramekins and other original items, as well as glass jars and bottles to fill with candy, cookies, nuts, spiced vinegars or flowers.

- Fill terra cotta flower pots with candy "pebbles" (such as chocolate M&M's) and "plant" a flower cookie attached to a bamboo stick or green garden stick. Or fill tiny pots with flowers, plants or herbs. As mentioned earlier, these pots can be sprayed or painted by hand, left plain or decorated with designs or ribbon.

- Unusual individual votives make nice favors. Include the candles, and light them to add to your table candlepower.

- If your budget allows you to splurge, look for silver boxes, limoges boxes, silver calendars and picture frames. Keep your eyes open while shopping and traveling.

- Picture frames don't have to display only pictures. Guest's names may be slipped inside – or appropriate messages, dried flowers, tiny paintings or pictures cut from magazines. Use miniature wallpaper (from doll house stores) for your matting.

- Spray paint wishbones you have collected silver or gold (or any color which will highlight your color scheme) or appropriate colors for holidays. Tie a contrasting bow around each one and attach a place card. At the end of the meal, the guests might use the wishbones to make individual wishes.

- Write guests' names on plain Christmas or hand-decorated ornaments. Ask your art store which pen or paint will work best. When decorating the ornament, leave enough room for the name, then attach a thin ribbon bow to the hanger loop.

- Small Christmas stockings make wonderful favors for the table or attached to the backs of chairs. If they don't come with hangers, add them by sewing on wide strips of felt or heavy ribbon, such as velvet. Fill them with food items or small gifts obtained from stationery or hardware stores. Take the time to individually wrap each item in the stockings.

- Interesting memo pads with the guest's name written across the first page are fun and useful favors. You might wish to include a pen or pencil. Animal shapes (such as rabbits and chicks found at Easter) may be used as the favor, or use a single sheet from the pad as the place card and attach it with a bow to a separate favor (see photograph on page 98.

- For baby showers, use baby bottles as "vases" (save the nipples and caps to give to the mother-to-be after the party). Use small ones for individual places and larger ones for the centerpiece. Fill the short bottles with small flowers and the taller bottles with long-stemmed flowers, or set them in a garland of ivy or other greenery. If both large and small sized bottles are used as the centerpiece, give each guest a baby bracelet (found in stores that sell dolls) with her name on it as a place card.

- Fill empty, clean baby food jars with candy or nuts. Try to keep the labels intact while washing the jars, or if you want the labels removed, paint the tops pink, blue, yellow or green. Tie a thin ribbon, with place card attached, around the jar, or glue a bow to the top and leave the place card unattached.

- A novel idea for a favor would be to put a baby picture of your guests, if you could obtain them, in small picture frames and use them as place cards.

- For international and bon voyage parties, choose your favors and accessories from small maps, globes, travel brochures, foreign currency, travel diaries and the flags, foods and beverages of the countries being highlighted. International markets and gift shops will provide a wealth of ideas and inspiration.

Party Poppers

Party Poppers are easy to make, colorful and fun additions to any party table setting. They can be purchased at party stores or through some catalogs, but you can easily make your own. All you need are some paper towel tubes, some covering material (colored or gilt gift wrapping paper), scissors, pinking shears, rubber cement, ribbon and some small surprises as "fillers" (small toys, candy, money, individual horoscopes, jokes or games).

To make your Party Poppers, cut the towel tubes into sections about *five inches long*. Cut the covering material into *six inch wide* strips *fifteen inches long* using pinking shears. Lay the covering material face down and "paint" the back surface with rubber cement. Center the tube sections on the covering material and roll them up, being certain that the seam is well glued. Fill the tube with the "fillers," and tie the ends closed with ribbon. The illustration on the following page shows how this is done. When completed, put one at each place setting as a favor or a favor/place card.

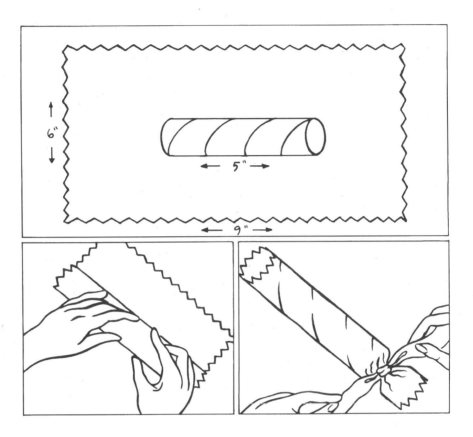

Instructions for making Party Poppers

The finished Party Poppers

Handicraft Materials

Set aside a drawer or a corner in a closet which has room for large, lidded boxes for your party supplies and materials. Start collecting now in order to have things on hand when you need them to make place mats, napkins, place cards or favors. I suggest that you stow away the following when you happen to find something that interests you while shopping or marketing (you may even have a number of these items already on hand):

- colored papers – these usually come in packages or tablets

- colored pens

- colored yarns

- dried flowers

- empty coffee cans and candy boxes

- fabric pieces – save the old dress or sheet that has an interesting pattern to cover boxes, cans, flower holders, favors or food containers

- glitter

- glue – rubber cement, Glue Bird, glue stick

- glue gun – particularly useful for precision gluing decorations on cards, boxes, cans or wreaths

- hole punch

- jewels, sequins, pearls, beads and beading

- lace – lace ribbon, pieces of lace

- lollipop or ice cream sticks

- needlepoint needle – this is an alternative to a hole punch, and would be used to pull a thin ribbon through place cards

- paper cutter, small – for professionally cutting place cards and matting

- plain Christmas balls – red, green, silver, gold, white, clear

- ribbons, wire ribbon and rickrack – save used ribbons; when ironed they look like new (to make your own wire ribbon, place a thin wire between two layers of ribbon and glue them together)

- scissors – several sizes plus pinking shears

- Scotch tape – including double stick tape for use in wrapping gifts and favors

- seashells – collected during trips to the beach or purchased at a variety store

- small ruler and yardstick

- spray paint

- stapler

- tiny baskets and boxes

- tiny empty jam and jelly jars

- tissue paper – both white and colored

- unusual invitations – when discovered, buy enough for a party of 10 to 20 (they might even inspire you to have a party)

- unused cards and notepaper – unusual ones, if blank inside, may be used for invitations

- wrapping paper – wonderful coverings for boxes, jars and cans (as with ribbons, used wrapping paper can be carefully ironed flat to remove the wrinkles)

Sources

Once in a while, a question arises as to where to find the materials needed for entertaining. Sources have been suggested throughout this book, but for quick reference many are listed below:

- **Art supply stores** – paints, colored pens, pencils, colored paper, gold and silver leaf to decorate cakes and cookies, "clip art" books (see page 34 for more about "clip art")

- **Antique stores** – special gifts, containers

- **Bath shops** – small soaps for gifts, apothecary jars for food and flowers

- **Bookstores** – another good source for "clip art" books, party games

- **Boutiques** – small gifts, unusual invitations

- **Cooking stores** – foods, small containers

- **Craft and hobby stores** – materials for decorating favors

- **Department stores** – table tops, linens, kitchenware

- **Discount stores** – party goods and supplies, favors, food and tableware

- **Ethnic and international stores** – gold and silver leaf to decorate your cakes and candies can be found in most East Indian markets, ideas for favors and gifts, food containers

- **Fabric stores** – ribbon, lace, fabric, buttons, sequins, doweling

- **Floral supply stores** – silk, paper flowers, Styrofoam, decorating materials, ribbon, ornaments, paper goods, containers of all kinds, floral tape and wire

- **Florists** – cut flower water vials, oasis, vases

- **Hardware stores** – small gifts, glue, paint

- **Lumber yards** – if you need doweling from which to hang objects, or if you need stands or bases, you will generally find friendly help in cutting just the right sizes and shapes that you need

- **Markets** – nuts, candy, small aluminum bread pans, food and paper goods

- **Miniature stores** – doll house wallpaper, decorations

- **Nurseries and garden stores** – flowers, containers for food and flowers, oasis

- **Party shops** – paper and plastic plates, centerpieces, decorations, cloths, glassware and eating utensils; accessories, such as leis for Hawaiian parties, flags and balloons for bon voyage parties; supplies for children's parties and very informal outdoor picnics, barbecues and luncheons

- **Stationery stores** – a good source for invitations, place cards, "clip art" books, pens, pencils, picture frames, gift items and miniature books

- **Swap meets and garage sales** – furniture, dishware, linens, food and flower containers

- **Toy stores** – sand pails, boats, hats, masks, games, animals, small books

"Clip Art" books are books or pamphlets of nearly every design and decoration imaginable, which you can clip out and use for decorating invitations, place cards and favors. Once the design has been clipped from the book, it can be glued to a plain piece of paper, taken to a local print shop, enlarged or reduced, and printed in whatever color you want.

Catalogs

For wonderful hours of "armchair shopping," pick up the phone and order these catalogs which are favorites of mine, and which I use all the time. They will provide you with an amazing array of products, and they will kindle your enthusiasm for party planning.

CRATE & BARREL – (800) 323-5461
cookware, dishes, dining accessories

CURRENT, INC. – (800) 525-7170
cards, invitations, punches, recipe cards

GARDENERS EDAN – (800) 822-9600
gifts, accessories, furniture

HORCHOW COLLECTION – (800) 456-7000
gifts, favors, dining accessories

LILLIAN VERNON – (800) 285-5555
gifts, favors, rubber stamps, punches, etc.

MAID OF SCANDINAVIA – (800) 328-6722
baking and candy making tools, molds

MYACAMAS FINE FOODS – (707) 996-0955
herbs, mixes for sauces, salads, dips

PARAGON, THE – (800) 343-3095
gifts, favors, rubber stamps, punches, etc.

STUMPS – (800) 342-5644
party decorations and props

TRIFLES – (800) 456-7019
gifts, favors, dining accessories

WILLIAMS-SONOMA – (800) 541-2233
cookware, dishes, dining accessories

PARTY THEMES AND TYPES OF PARTIES

The opportunities for entertaining are endless. Sprinkled throughout the four seasons of the year are birthdays, anniversaries, bon voyages, teas, garden parties, barbecues, formal and informal dinners.

The occasion will establish the theme of the party, and that theme should set the stage for all of the details – the setting, the invitations, the decorations, the favors, the menu and even the guest list. The weather will certainly play a major role in determining the kind of party you have, but most other variables are totally in your control.

Through thoughtful planning and implementation, you can graciously honor friends or family members by celebrating a birthday, a wedding, a trip, or by just bringing good friends and family together for informal fun and the opportunity to see one another more often.

The choice of occasion is all yours. Do as you wish, how you wish, and with whom you wish.

My hope is that with the suggestions and advice found within these pages you will find, as I have, that you can relax and enjoy giving parties – both formal and elegant or informal and casual – with a wide and varied array of dishes, decorations, and menus to choose from. The key to success, pampering both your guests and yourself, is advance planning and advance preparation.

In this chapter I have outlined a variety of party suggestions from traditional holiday celebrations to gatherings for specific events.

These suggestions are not intended to be all encompassing, nor do they attempt to cover all holidays. I do not want you to feel that you must do everything that I have suggested – they are offered only as a catalyst to stimulate your thinking. It is my hope that you will add your ideas and creativity to achieve your own personal style of entertaining.

You will find that in the suggested party themes which follow, I have devoted a lot of time to some and spent little time on others. This is simply by choice and is a reflection of my own prior experience.

I hope you will read these suggestions with the same enthusiasm with which I write them, and use them as a guide for your own party successes.

With each entertaining endeavor you undertake, you will become increasingly more at ease and creative. You will feel happy and fulfilled, even proud, once you have begun.

Entertaining family and friends in your home, in your own personal way, is well worth all the love and effort that you will put into it, and your guests will abundantly reward you for that effort.

For reference, some events which are great opportunities for giving parties are:

SPRING (begins March 20th)

> *March*
> 17th – Saint Patrick's Day
>
> *April*
> Easter (sometimes in late March)
> Teas and garden parties
>
> *May*
> First Saturday – Kentucky Derby Day
> 5th – Cinco de Mayo
> Second Sunday – Mother's Day
> 30th – Memorial Day

SUMMER (begins June 20th)

> *June*
> 3rd Sunday – Father's Day
> Commencement Day
> Brides' month
>
> *July*
> 4th – Fourth of July
>
> *August*
> Picnics, barbecues, beach, swimming and garden parties

FALL (begins September 22nd)

> *September*
> 1st Monday – Labor Day
> Back to school
> Picnics, barbecues, beach, swimming and garden parties

October
12th – Columbus Day
31st – Halloween (possibly a costume party)

November
2nd Tuesday – Election Day
Last Thursday – Thanksgiving

WINTER (begins December 21st)

December
25th – Christmas
31st – New Year's Eve

January
1st – New Year's Day (big game day)

February
Chinese New Year (sometimes late January)
12th – Lincoln's Birthday
14th – Valentine's Day
22nd – Washington's Birthday

Other Themes and Occasions

In addition to the above events which make great opportunities for giving parties, the following list of additional *events and occasions* may serve as a check list to aid in your planning:

- beach or nautical
- circus
- regional (western, southern, eastern, northern)
- international travel
- bridge or other games
- oscar night
- a night at the movies
- adult "Children's" party

- anniversary
- fondue
- after (tennis, sailing, swimming) party
- baby shower
- birthday
- neighborhood get-together
- pampered pet party (for those of us who have pampered pets)
- garden party
- picnic
- barbecue
- astrological
- retirement
- black and white night (formal dinner wear)

There. are many different *types of parties* you can give for most of the above events, some of which are:

- cocktail buffets
- grazing (hearty appetizers and desserts)
- teas
- brunches
- luncheons
- formal or informal
- buffet or sit-down

If you are considering a *bridal shower*, there are any number of themes to choose from, some of which are:

- kitchen
- bed and bath
- lingerie
- garden – the men can be included
- barbecue – the men can be included
- bar – the men can be included
- paper
- china/pottery/crystal
- linen
- recipe (bring a dish or ingredients)
- around the clock – assign each guest a time
- around the house – assign each guest a room

- month of the year – assign each guest a month
- Christmas (ornaments, china, glassware)
- entertainment (tapes, videos, sporting goods)
- cookware
- miscellaneous

Types of Parties for Holidays and Special Occasions

In the following pages of this chapter, I will outline the elements of a variety of parties I have given or attended, which illustrate many of the above party themes or situations. These are offered to stimulate your own creativity and thinking and are not, in any way, intended to include all possible themes and occasions.

Potluck Party (It's Everybody's Party)

This is one of the easiest and simplest kinds of parties to have. You don't have to do all the cooking, thus you can focus your attention on practicing your presentation skills.

This type of party is a good way to bring family and good friends together often. You can share your favorite foods and recipes, whether you make your contribution yourself or purchase it from a market. Either way, you will have fun doing the party, especially if the atmosphere is relaxed. The most important consideration is bringing people together; the bill of fare is a secondary consideration. Your menu can include appetizers (just nuts and popcorn is perfectly acceptable), a meat dish or casserole, salads and/or a vegetable, breads or muffins, and dessert.

As the host or hostess, you choose the main dish you want to serve and have your guests bring complementary dishes. If you have planned a very large event, you might wish to have several choices in each category. Also as hostess, you are responsible for the predinner cocktails and dinner beverages.

My editor and I are members of a small potluck group, and for one dinner occasion she brought the salad – a large bowl of mixed greens, tossed with an oil and vinegar dressing, and surrounded by bowls of various salad condiments (chopped mushrooms, radishes, avocado, green onions, tomatoes, cucumber, hard-boiled eggs, crumbled bacon, croutons, etc.) like a salad bar.

Your guests should feel comfortable with the dish they are asked to bring, and if possible you should allow them a choice. It's up to you, as the party giver, to coordinate the food so there is a balanced selection pleasing to both the palate and the eye.

If you don't have time to do the flowers, ask an invited guest with a bountiful garden to help you by providing the flowers and assisting in the arrangements. This would take the place of bringing a dish. Or you can call on your local florist for help.

Plan the party according to type (buffet or sit-down), theme (if any), location (garden or indoors), and budget. You can make a potluck casual and use paper plates, or you can make it as formal as you like. If you tend towards the formal, this is the time to get out your beautiful fine china and best crystal.

Weather permitting, an informal location to hold your potluck is outside – a barbecue or picnic on the porch, balcony, lawn or in the garden. If the ground is to be your "table," don't forget to have plenty of candles (protected, of course) for added atmosphere.

For a warm and wonderful indoor meal, plan a simple and light-hearted supper around a hearty soup and set it up by the fire. If the idea appeals to you, bake your own bread – your guests can bring the appetizers, salads and desserts.

Buy a book on bread making if you are new at it. Don't be afraid to work with yeast, just be sure that it is fresh by checking the date on the package, and that the water temperature in which you dissolve it is between 105° and 115° Farenheidt. Baking bread is fun, and the end product is most rewarding. Just watching the soft dough rise, and

experiencing the aroma and taste of a slice of warm, buttered, freshly baked bread is reason enough to try it. Or if you want, try rolls.

Set up card tables, or collapsible tables, and chairs near the fireplace and allow the guests to sit where they are most comfortable – on the floor, if they wish, in which case the soup should be served in a mug. This is easier to handle when balancing a plate on your lap. You might want to set out both mugs and bowls so your guests can make their own choice.

Encourage guests to bring their assigned food contributions in attractive serving dishes. This will create less fuss for you – you will be busy enough taking care of all the details before, during and after the party.

Cheese Fondue Party

In keeping with the theme, try covering tables in yellow, orange and white fabric – plain, plaids, or stripes, with matching or contrasting napkins.

In the center of each table, place a fondue pot, or a chafing dish, filled with the cheese dip. Pass bread cubes and serve with a green salad and a light dessert (see Holland Party Theme, page 179).

For favors, place a small package of cheese at each place. Cut out a daisy-like flower from colored paper, tracing over the templet provided on the next page, and glue it to a toothpick. Write the guest's name on the "daisy," glue or Scotch tape the toothpick to the back of the cheese package, and you have your place card!

If you are a collector of cow paraphernalia, now is the time to display it and bring a touch of black into your color scheme. This kind of party is generally very casual, a lot of fun, and very easy on the budget.

*Templet (pattern) for making daisies from colored paper for
place cards or from dough for cookies*

Children's Party

Instead of playing games, give each child a picture frame, either paper or wood, or some plain small boxes or cans to decorate. Buy lots of stickers, colored paper, glitter, etc. Have bits of fabric to cut out and glue on the items to be decorated.

If using picture frames, borrow a Polaroid and take a picture of each child, or the group of guests, to put in his or her frame. If using boxes or cans, fill them with candy. Children love taking home things they have made.

Adult "Children's" Birthday Party

A good friend of mine wanted to do something fun and different for her husband who was turning 60. Her idea was to have a children's party for adults, so she sent out invitations to a "6(0)th" birthday party. Each guest was encouraged to bring a toy as a present, and to dress in kiddy style (though not necessarily at the six year old level).

She cooked hamburgers and hot dogs on the barbecue and served popcorn and pretzels in little red wagons and firemen's hats she had found at a toy store. The centerpieces were adorned with all-day suckers and helium-filled balloons. At each place she had filled a colorful little tote bag with games, pencils and paper, and paper hats.

Before dinner, the guests played "pin the tail on the donkey," and took swings with a baseball bat at a colorful rooster piñata filled with candies and chewing gum.

Birthday Book Party

I gave this party for my hard-working editor, and although I hosted it at a local club, the idea proved to be successful. For a gift, I asked each guest to bring a copy of a favorite book, short story or poem. It was interesting to see the variety.

For favors, I found miniature books – and miniature bookmarks as well – at the bookstore. There were so many titles offered that I was able to hand pick the category I thought would best fit each guest. I placed the miniature books and bookmarks in small floral tote bags lined with colored tissue paper, and ordered a colorful centerpiece from the florist which I gave to the honored guest to take home. With dessert, we toasted the birthday girl with champagne in icy cold, frosted glasses.

Swiss Birthday Party Custom

A delightful birthday custom observed by a Swiss family I know is to place a floral "halo" at the birthday honoree's place at the table. A "necklace" of small flowers or flower petals adorns the place mat at the top of the place setting.

Beach/Nautical/Tropical Party

There are a myriad of props available for rent or purchase which will make your party a real success. Rent small palm trees from your nursery. Sand may be purchased from the nursery or a building supply store. However, unless you are entertaining at the beach, bringing in a lot of sand is a bit tricky and very messy! Perhaps your children have a sandbox that you could use as a prop.

Import and/or party stores carry tiki torches, hurricane globes to shelter candles, goldfish bowls, glass floats, fishnetting, leis and tiny parasols to decorate tropical drinks (see Catalogs – Stumps, page 35).

Toy stores might provide you with small boats as well as multi-colored sand pails. The smaller pails can be partially filled with sand and used to hold flowers or votive candles (placed in the center away from the sides). The larger ones can be filled with all kinds of food – nuts, popcorn, pretzels – or used as serving dishes for salads and cookies, or as soft drink and wine coolers.

If you have a pool or spa, float toy boats in it. Borrow (or rent) small sails, rope, anchors and surfboards to use as props around the house and yard. Nautical flags and port (red) and starboard (green) lights may be difficult to come by, but they make great additions to a nautical motif. Collect seashells from the beach, or if you are near a seaside town, check the Yellow Pages under *shells* for stores which sell them. Use them for dips, salters (salt dishes) or votive holders.

For centerpieces, fill clear glass containers with goldfish or fighting fish (but not both together in one container) and surround them with houseplants and ferns, colored glass balls (floats), shells and heavy fishnetting. Glass hurricanes provide the perfect lighting.

Barbecued or baked sweet-and-sour chicken and spareribs combine to make a perfect menu when accompanied by a green salad and muffins or French bread. A wonderful flaming dessert recipe my husband and I brought back from our honeymoon in Hawaii teamed papaya with coffee ice cream (see Hawaiian Party Theme, page 175).

Cover your tables with straw matting, taro (batik) cloth strips, fishnetting, etc., and for napkins use fabric with tropical or nautical designs. For favors, cover small boxes with the same fabric or fill fabric bags or miniature sand pails with candy or nuts, and add a raffia bow or tie. You can also place a lei, made from real or paper flowers, at each place. Play Hawaiian music or music of the sea on the CD player or stereo.

Western Party

My husband and I combined ideas with another couple for a western party, and the end result was very successful. The men went to a local pet store and picked up several bales of straw which we placed on the lawn. *For fire prevention, you should spray the straw with a fire retardant and keep candles and other fire sources well away from it.* Your local hardware store probably carries an appropriate fire retardant; if not, consult the fire department

We hired a three-piece western combo right out of the Yellow Pages under *Musicians,* and since the evening was obviously going to be noisy, warned the neighbors.

We rented dishes from a party supply store and purchased Mason-type jars at the market which we used for glasses. For favors, we decorated Shaker-type boxes and filled them with chocolate guns and western hats made from plastic candy molds. Again, using the Yellow Pages (under *Popcorn*), we rented a popcorn machine, and through a friend located a man with an old-fashioned ice cream cart to serve up a variety of ice cream cones for dessert.

The tables were covered with a potpourri of colored cotton cloths, although oilcloth or denim would work as well. If you don't want to cover your tables, use straw place mats instead of tablecloths.

For napkins, we bought large bandannas we had found in catalogs and in the men's section of a local department store and tied them with raffia. During the party, some guests tied them around their small waists, made them into headbands, or tucked them into their hip pockets; later, the guests took them home as a memento of the evening. If you have time, you could make your own napkins from denim or gingham. Tie your napkins with raffia or tie them in a loose self-knot.

For the bases of the centerpieces, we bought Styrofoam rounds and "painted" them with a household glue, then covered them with hay and sand. We purchased miniature horses at the toy store and placed one on each round. We found straw-like flowers and weeds on a walk around the neighborhood and stuck them in and around the horses to look like trees and shrubbery. The photograph on page 84 highlights the miniature horse centerpiece made with Styrofoam and straw, decorated boxes with molded chocolate guns and hats as favors, and Mason-type jar "glasses."

Blue splatterware tin cups and pots served as flower vases and food containers. We filled western hats with popcorn and pretzels, muffins and cookies (they may also be used to hold flowers for centerpieces).

For dinner we served chili in individual bowls, which we had rented (see *Party Supplies* in the Yellow Pages), accompanied by a green salad and cornbread. We had ice cream cones, served from the old-fashioned ice cream cart, and cookies for dessert. "Mud pies" – chocolate cookie crust filled with coffee ice cream topped with chocolate sauce – would also go well with this menu.

In lieu of a band, play taped western music ("*Home on the Range*," "*I'm an Old Cowhand*," etc.) and have your guests do the potato dance (see *Games*, page 12). If you have a large back yard and an adequate budget, you might want to satisfy the child that's within all of us and rent a pony for a few hours. Take pictures of your guests either on the pony or beside it. Have an extra prop or two (bandanna, cowboy hat, rope, etc.) on hand for the pictures, just in case they are needed.

Mexican Fiesta

The red and green colors of the Mexican flag make them the perfect choice for a Christmas fiesta or dinner party. In the southwest, piñatas are found in Mexican specialty stores year 'round, but they are especially festive at Christmas time. As a focal point for a Mexican fiesta, piñatas are loved by both children and adults alike.

Use green and red tablecloths with contrasting colored napkins (i.e., red napkins on a green tablecloth). For your centerpiece, tall red and green candles, protected by hurricane globes found in lighting stores, are perfect. Set them inside a wreath or surround them with Christmas greens. For favors, give each guest red and green boxes, jars or miniature paper bags filled with cookies, candy or nuts. Mexican Christmas ornaments found at folk art stores or import stores are most appropriate if you have time to look around and find which ones fit your budget. Tie the ornaments to the boxes, jars or paper bags along with a place card.

For an appetizer, serve a layered Mexican dip or guacamole with tostada chips (see Mexican Party Theme, page 161). If you have time, go to a Mexican restaurant and buy their guacamole and chips – both freeze well. If you'd rather, make your own, or purchase them at the market. If you get your guacamole at the market, add a little salsa and diced fresh avocado, and everybody will think you made it yourself.

A good menu might consist of chicken or beef enchiladas, or steak (beef fillets) and mini quesadillas (see page 163) and a green salad. And for dessert, a tequila sorbet or creamy flan (see page 165). If you don't want to make the flan yourself, try your favorite Mexican restaurant, or purchase boxed Knorr's Creme Caramel in the gourmet food section of your market – but be sure to enrich it with a little half-and-half or cream.

Depending on the size of your party and your budget, you might want to hire a mariachi band to play during dinner or throughout the evening. If this is a Christmas party, be sure to include traditional Christmas carols.

A Night at the Movies

My nephew hosted this wonderful party! Instead of name tags, he used black and white labels resembling strips of movie film. The name of the movie to be shown that evening (Mame!) was printed at the top; in the center the word "Starring" was followed by a space for writing in each guest's name. This is what my name tag looked like:

It was an informal affair, with cocktails followed by an easy buffet of fresh vegetables with a variety of dips; pasta salads; cheeses; and platters of ham, turkey and roast beef for make-your-own sandwiches. All of this was set out on the dining room table. Several types of large dinner rolls were split, buttered, and then piled into baskets.

Additional butter, mayonnaise and assorted mustards were attractively presented, along with beautiful pastries and cookies.

A large screen was set up in the garden along with a projector, appropriately positioned for viewing but out of the way of the guests. Both the screen and the projector were rented from sources found in the Yellow Pages under *Photography and Cameras*. Folding chairs, also rented, were set up in rows. After dinner, while the movie was being shown, attentive helpers passed individually filled bags of popcorn and trays of candy bars. It was an evening to remember.

If you prefer to move your "Night at the Movies" inside, the same effect can be achieved (but on a smaller scale) with a giant television screen and a good video.

Oscar Night Party

Many of us are glued to the television on Oscar Night. We always hope that our favorites will be among the winners chosen by the Motion Picture Academy of Arts and Sciences.

If possible, have several television sets (borrowed or rented) placed around the house so your guests can wander from room to room without missing any of the action. It is best to locate the bar in one room and serve a simple buffet in another. This will improve the circulation flow and avoid congestion. Also, it will make it possible for your guests to either sit and watch TV during dinner or circulate with plate in hand if they prefer.

Make ballot cards for the top nominees (handmade or printed by your local print shop) and enclose them with the invitations. Ask your guests to mark their ballots beforehand. Have a basket by the door where they can deposit them as they arrive.

For those who correctly pick the winners, give prizes such as movie cassettes, movie passes, magazines, newspapers or books (paperback autobiographies of nominated movie personalities, history of movies, etc.), depending upon your budget. Trophy shops often have miniature trophies or Oscars. Be prepared for more than one winner.

Cut out stars for name tags or put star stickers on plain white name tags. An Oscar Night might be the perfect occasion to have a potluck buffet. Ask each guest to bring a dish named after one of the movies (*Fried Green Tomatoes,* etc.) or a movie star (Clint Eastwood's chili, green salad with Paul Newman's dressing, etc.). Put on your creative thinking cap!

Bridal Shower Luncheon

Start your party early and plan to have the bride-to-be open her gifts before lunch. You don't want to feel rushed, and often some of the guests will need to leave soon after the luncheon.

Don't forget the traditional paper plate which will make the base for the ribbon bouquet the bride-to-be will carry at the wedding rehearsal. Make two cross slits in the center of a large paper plate and pull through the trailers of the bows from gift wrappings. You might advise the bride to be careful as she opens presents, since there is an old superstition that a baby will be born for each ribbon that is broken.

You will need two volunteers: one to make the ribbon bouquet, and one to make a list of the gifts received and who they are from. Have a pad of paper and pencil on hand to record this important information.

Place a pretty floral centerpiece on each table. Combine different varieties and shades of white flowers, or depending on the time of year, fill bowls or baskets with a variety of colors to match your napkins, place mats or tablecloths.

If you are using your own (or borrowed) containers for the floral arrangements, have your florist (or you can do it yourself) fit a sturdy inner liner into one of them. That way the arrangement can be lifted out and given to the bride-to-be to take home.

For a kitchen shower, fill a nested set of mixing bowls with the floral arrangements and give them to the bride-to-be to take home after the party. Use the largest bowl for the bridal table centerpiece, and the smaller ones as centerpieces for the other tables. In each centerpiece, along with the flowers, stick in small kitchen utensils such as spatulas, measuring spoons, melon ballers, pizza cutters, etc. If using a florist, ask him to do this for you. I had one florist who, much to my delight, added picnic salts and peppers and pretzels glued or taped to wooden skewers.

For favors, I have given the guests miniature porcelain baskets and pitchers filled with candy; small wicker baskets filled with little jars of jams and mustards; individual and unusual kitchen accessories; miniature bottles filled with herbal vinegars with a tiny recipe attached. Small bags of potpourri, soaps and lotions or handkerchiefs and sachets also make nice favors, especially for linen, miscellaneous and bath showers.

Tie place cards to any of the items mentioned above. If you have a favorite poem or saying that is appropriate for the occasion, have it printed on individual cards or sheets of paper, roll it up and tie with a narrow ribbon. These cards or scrolls can also be used as place cards.

For a luncheon menu, salads are always popular. There are many varieties of salads to choose from: fruit, vegetable, chicken, seafood, and gelatin, to name only a few. Serve two or three kinds on each plate, a chicken or seafood and a vegetable or fruit, with an addition of deviled eggs decorated with edible flowers such as violas or geraniums (see Luncheon Menu Suggestions, page 143 and illustration on page 91). If the weather is cold, you might want to serve a hot quiche with a tossed green salad.

Make or buy muffins or tiny croissants.

For dessert, serve individual tarts, cakes or mousses. I serve a chocolate mousse in my miscellaneous collection of demitasse cups. Have iced tea, mineral water and wine available for prelunch cocktails and luncheon beverages.

Anniversary/Engagement Party

This is the perfect time to get out your best silver and crystal dishes, bowls, vases, etc. Look around your house or borrow from friends; make a trip to the flea markets or antique stores where you might find a bargain which will just "fit the bill" for this very special party.

Fill these pretty containers, large and small, with food and flowers. It doesn't matter how the containers are customarily used; if they can be effective in your overall scheme, use them!

You might want to use a combination of all white flowers for this occasion. Depending on the season, there are many varieties to choose from. I love Queen Anne's lace mixed with roses or tulips. Cover your tables with white damask or lace cloths or mats.

For a different look, spray straw mats with silver paint. Slip napkins through silver or lacy white napkin rings (which you can make yourself if you wish), or just tie a ribbon around each one.

For the budget conscious, cut rings one to three inches wide from stiff wrapping paper tubes which you have saved. Spray them inside and out with silver or white paint and decorate with ribbon or lace. Glue the ribbon all the way around, inside and out, for a finished look.

Use lots of candlelight. Table mirrors to reflect the glow of the candles are very effective. Look for them in linen stores or wherever dining accessories are available; you may even find them at your florist.

For favors, scout around for silver baskets or boxes, or try spraying or covering your own boxes with paint or paper. Purchase inexpensive, small picture frames to hold photographs or love poems. Look for mini calendars (if the cover is not to your liking, cover it with a light fabric or paper). Glue a star to the wedding date, and mark the page with a ribbon.

For the couple being honored, put together a small scrapbook of old photographs which you have collected from friends and from your own albums. Or have each guest contribute to the purchase of a silver

box and fill it with a "memories" note from each guest. Have the box engraved with the honorees' names and the date of the party or the date of the wedding.

Any of these gifts may be presented with a flourish of congratulatory toasts to the honored couple during dessert and champagne. Borrow a Polaroid if you don't have one, and send everyone home with a memento of the evening.

A special occasion deserves a special menu, such as individual filets mignons or chicken wrapped in filo. At dessert time, serve champagne and a beautifully decorated cake or ice cream in lacy cookie cups topped with chocolate candy hearts.

The following are suggestions for party favors for a few selected anniversaries:

> *1st year* – **paper**: decorative notepads, magazine
> subscriptions, mini books, calendars

> *5th year* – **wood**: boxes filled with candy or nuts,
> picture frames

> *10th year* – **tin or aluminum**: boxes or cans filled
> with candy or nuts

> *15th year* – **crystal**: glass containers, vases, votives filled
> with mini floral bouquets

> *20th year* – **china**: vases, ramekins or pitchers
> holding flowers, candy or nuts

> *25th year* – **silver**: spray boxes and frames silver
> or purchase small items of silver

> *50th year* – **gold**: spray boxes and frames gold
> or purchase small items of gold

Astrological Party

Using your own imagination, decorate your tables, food and favors with stars, suns and moons. Use shades of blue, yellow, silver or gold.

Buy, or obtain from your local library, Linda Goodwin's book *Sun Signs* and create individual "fortunes" for your guests using their birth dates. Roll the written or printed fortunes into a scroll, tie with a thin ribbon, and attach a small place card to the ribbon.

Palm readers or tarot card readers are always popular – look for them in the Yellow Pages under *Entertainment*. Game stores might provide you with additional ideas.

Astrological shaped molds and cookie cutters for appetizers and desserts are available at kitchenware stores. Fabric and stationery stores can provide you with materials and decorations highlighting stars, suns and moons. A good time to have an astrological party is in the summer when it is warm. Invite your guests to dine with you beneath the stars!

Garden Party

A beautiful garden makes a delightful dining room. This is particularly true if your garden, be it large or small, is filled with a profusion of flowers or is lush with green foliage. A pool is a glamorous added attraction should you have one.

There are a number of important things to consider in planning any outdoor party. First: you must be prepared to bring the party indoors if the weather has an abrupt change of mind. Always have an alternative plan in mind – remember, all of your guests will be well aware of the weather and won't hold it against you, so make light of the necessary change.

Second: in addition to housework, you will probably need to do some yard work. Unless you have a gardener, you will have to determine how much time you will have available for clipping, planting and weeding – but as a minimum, someone should sweep and wash down the patio and walkways shortly before the party. Washing down not only makes everything look and smell fresh, but it helps to keep the bugs away and may prevent a guest from slipping on a leaf or a small rock on a pathway. Also, be sure that someone rakes the lawn or it will distract from the rest of your planting. And as you would arrange flowers inside, you may feel the need to add more flowering plants outside for color. Put them in inexpensive terra cotta pots and place them in groups on the patio or around the yard.

Third: for your guests' comfort on hot sticky days, you might want to have some insect repellent, sun hats, sunscreen and a few pairs of dark glasses on hand for their use during the day. Also have some sweaters available for evening affairs, since cold breezes might come up unexpectedly after a very warm day.

Citronella candles, which ward off mosquitoes and other flying insects, are available in all colors and kinds of containers. Catalogs and garden centers carry citronella pots for tables and tiki torches to stick into the ground or potted plants. *Be sure to place these torches well away from foliage and buildings, and that all candles are protected inside votives or glass hurricane globes.*

Luminarios (decorative paper sacks half-filled with sand with a votive candle set in the center) make excellent and unique lighting for driveways and front steps, and are becoming more and more popular. They can be found in a variety of colors and designs in many catalogs and specialty stores.

If you are going to serve food outside, be sure it is covered with gauze "umbrellas," lids or other plastic wraps to protect it from flying insects and bugs. Also, check to see that food tables are away from trees shedding leaves.

For daytime parties, be sure you don't leave food that can spoil (seafood, chicken, uncooked fish, anything with mayonnaise in it, etc.) sitting in the heat unless it is protected with crushed ice, ice cubes or dry ice. It is best to leave such foods in the refrigerator until the very last minute, and as an added precaution, you may decide to serve those foods from a buffet inside and let your guests take their plates outside for the rest of the meal.

If your garden is small, filling terra cotta pots with flowers and placing them inside the house brings your garden indoors and amplifies the total effect. They also make unique centerpieces, and miniature versions can be used as individual favors. Another centerpiece idea is to make a wreath, using hairpins to attach ivy, other greens and flowers to Styrofoam, and set a candle protected with a glass hurricane in the center. A table setting for a garden party highlighting a terra cotta centerpiece, terra cotta favors and garden-accented place settings is pictured on page 88.

For an evening party, mini lights (or "twinkle lights") draped on trees and shrubs create a fairyland effect. Tiki torches are also effective for beach and barbecue parties, *but make sure their location does not pose a fire threat.* Also, floating candles in the pool provide a touch of fun and elegance.

If you have a rainbow of colorful flowers in your garden, accent them with plain tablecloths and feature a floral centerpiece.

Bridal Garden Shower

This is a good opportunity to entertain the groom as well as the bride-to-be, especially if gardening is their favorite pastime.

Fill watering cans, baskets and clay pots with flowers and plants. Use the clay pots, along with baskets, for finger foods such as appetizers, muffins, rolls, cookies and candy. Ice the bottled or canned drinks in wheelbarrows.

For favors, fill individual clay pots with flowers or herb plants. For a place card, glue a seed packet to a garden stick and insert it into the pot. To make matching centerpieces, fill containers with flowers or vegetables and add seed packets and gardening gloves for the honored guests to take home. Wrap napkins in garden twisty ties, raffia or

sprigs of fresh ivy. Place silverware in the fingers of gardening gloves and set them on plates or place mats.

A luncheon might include a cold vegetable platter and poached chicken, antipasto style, with a tonnato (tuna) aioli (garlic) sauce or dressing. For a fanciful dessert, line individual clay pots with foil and fill them with sherbets or sorbets topped with fresh fruit and sprinkled liberally with fruit cordials. Insert edible flowers, paper flowers, or candy flowers which have been "glued" to a bamboo stick. Pass a basket of flower-shaped cookies which you can make from ice box cookie dough using the daisy templet on page 45.

If you decide to have a dinner rather than a luncheon, start with a colorful appetizer such as a hollowed out cabbage or squash filled with your favorite dip for vegetables. Barbecue, bake or broil steak and top with mushrooms that have been lightly sautéed in butter and red wine. Accompany this with a vegetable lasagna or vegetable moussaka and either zucchini or carrot muffins. For dessert and favors, see above.

Adorn the garden area with votives and twinkle lights. You might also consider hanging paper lanterns which can be found in oriental shops.

Barbecue Party

A typically American cookout is a barbecue dinner featuring steak, hamburgers, turkey, chicken or pork, which weather permitting, you can enjoy during any season. With mouth-watering marinades, as well as mesquite and hickory flavored wood chips, you won't have any trouble pleasing the palates of your hungry guests.

If the weather is hot, a cool and refreshing way to serve canned and bottled drinks is from an ice-filled tub or wheelbarrow. Consider including individual bottles of wine, now available in four-packs at most markets and liquor stores. This is one style of party where paper plates are very acceptable if you choose to use them. Be sure that you have a "hideaway" in which to throw the trash, and a separate container in which to put non-throwaway dishes and utensils. Both may be picked up later. If your party is catered, this caution may not be necessary.

There are various cuts of meat, poultry, seafood and vegetables which can be cooked on the grill and served either as appetizers or as entrées. Everything is dependent upon the type of barbecue you plan and the size of your guest list. You might even need a second barbecue grill, one for the appetizers and one for the entrées.

To please a combination of children and adults, host a holiday picnic and serve juicy barbecued hamburgers and hot dogs along with an assortment of toppings. Accompany the hamburgers/hot dogs with a tossed green salad and finger food vegetables (sliced carrots, celery sticks, etc.). Serve ice cream and cookies or ice cream bars for dessert.

If your lawn area is large enough, spread cloths, rugs, blankets or country comforters on flat, dry ground. For a centerpiece, place a flower basket in the center, or off to one side. Purchase wicker "trays," line them with colorful napkins, give one to each guest to be used as his or her "table," and wrap the utensils in a napkin.

Serve salad in individual plastic containers. Add to each tray a small votive, that can't be easily tipped over, as a final touch of ambiance. If you are seated at tables, "favor" each guest with a tiny basket filled with candy, nuts or flowers.

Teas

This is the time to get out your prettiest china, glassware and linens.

Set your dining room table and a buffet with an array of teas, tea sandwiches, cakes, cookies, tiny muffins and scones, jams, jellies, curds, and clotted cream (generally available at establishments which carry British products), dotted with strawberries or raspberries.

Uncap a bottle of your finest sherry for sipping alone or for making sherry tea. Cut finger sandwiches in fanciful shapes and garnish with edible flowers as illustrated on page 91.

To make decorative candies, melt thin chocolate or pastel mints, pour into plastic molds (see Catalogs-Maid of Scandinavia, page 34) and refrigerate until firm.

Enhance your tables and serving trays with flowers. You can brighten up plain glassware or jars with lovely ribbons, and fill them with your most beautiful buds and blossoms (see photograph on page 93).

For a more intimate occasion, place your tea table or tables outside in the garden or in the living room by a crackling fire.

Chinese New Year Luncheon

Gung hay fat choy! This is Chinese for "wishing you more money," a salutation you will hear frequently between January 21st and February 19th, the period during which the Chinese New Year is celebrated.

Red (for happiness and prosperity) is the color of choice for clothing and decorations. You might wish to mention that thought on your invitations by suggesting that your guests wear something red – a dress, ribbon, necktie, scarf – but be sure and tell them why.

Narcissus (new life) is the favored flower, and its fragrance is said to attract good fairies. When planted in a basket or shallow dish, it makes a lovely centerpiece.

Rice symbolizes the staff of life in the Chinese culture, so you might wish to scatter a handful or so around the base of the centerpiece. Or fill several tiny sauce dishes or Chinese dipping dishes with it, and place them on the table around the centerpiece. Appropriate small dishes are easily found in many Oriental shops, party or import stores, such as Pier One.

Tiny fans tucked in amongst the flowers will lend the finishing touch to your centerpiece. They also make attractive place cards. Place a pair of chopsticks inside a napkin or lay them across the top of each place mat.

For favors, fill red boxes or bags with chocolate candy coins (see photograph of a firecracker box on page 97). If you wish to include real coins, be sure they are coins in the even amounts (10¢ or 50¢), since many Chinese consider coins in odd amounts to be bad luck.

The signs of the Oriental zodiac might suggest ideas for decorations and favors. This is a cycle of twelve animals which repeats itself in the same sequence every twelve years. 1995 is the year of the Boar (some say it is the year of the Pig); it will be followed in order by the year of the Rat, Ox, Tiger, Rabbit, Dragon, Snake, Horse, Goat, Monkey, Cock, and Dog. Then, in the year 2007, the sequence starts all over again with the year of the Boar.

Your local library carries books of Confucian sayings which can be attached to, or written on the inside of, your place cards. Treat yourself and a friend to a Chinatown visit. Look around for party ideas and items for accessories, favors, serving pieces, etc.

For lunch, serve your favorite Chinese chicken salad (the lettuce and green onions symbolize business growth). Substitute barbecued pork (for good luck) for the chicken, and add mandarin oranges (for good fortune). Serve spring rolls (for prosperity) whether homemade or bought. For dessert, purchase green tea ice cream from a Chinese market or restaurant and set long red candles on top of each serving to scare off evil spirits. And, of course, no Chinese meal is complete without fortune cookies.

Valentine's Day Party

Now is the time to bring forth the pink and red ribbon, white lace, paper doilies and old-fashioned stand-up cards.

For a luncheon, serve molded tomato aspic or fruit flavored red gelatin salads. For a dinner party, choose an appetizer such as tiny tomatoes or red pepper halves filled with shrimp or salmon mousse; or cut cheeses into heart shapes and serve them on heart shaped crackers.

For a wonderful entrée, wrap individual chicken breasts or fillets mignons in filo and place a frill made of filo or a heart cut from puff pastry on top of each. Serve these with a light cream sauce tinted with puréed red pepper or tomato paste. Bake muffins, pies and tarts in heart shaped pans.

As your guests arrive, pin the names of well known lovers on their backs and have them guess who they are by asking each other questions. Give the winner a chocolate heart as a prize. Play mood music on the stereo or CD player, and serve dinner by candlelight.

Saint Patrick's Day Party

For the Irish, Saint Patrick's Day heralds the beginning of Spring!

The stores are full of party ideas. The green and white color theme provides an opportunity to use houseplants for your centerpiece, or greenery from your garden arranged in a vase or basket. Shamrock plants can be purchased from garden stores or nurseries. For added color, fill in with white flowers of your choice.

Float helium-filled green and white balloons to the ceiling or attach them to the backs of the guests' chairs in the dining room. Before blowing up the balloons, place a gift certificate inside – redeemable for an ice cream cone at your favorite ice cream store.

If your party falls on the birthday of one of your guests, buy a green top hat at a party or stationery store for the birthday boy or girl. If you find a sturdy one, you might use it as the centerpiece "vase" or fill it with crackers, pretzels, popcorn, or nuts.

Purchase or make place cards using a shamrock motif. For favors, give each guest a tiny shamrock plant, which you can find at a nursery or florist. You can spray the plant container green or wrap it in green fabric or foil. You could also fill small white boxes or dishes with green and white candies or candy coated almonds. Paint small cans or boxes, or cover them with green and white fabric, and fill them with nuts.

A traditional dinner would be corned beef and cabbage with boiled potatoes sprinkled with parsley. Or you might try my favorite, Irish stew served in bread bowls (see Irish Party Theme, page 167). Add a tossed green salad, and you have an easy and delicious meal. For dessert, a key lime pie, pistachio ice cream, or vanilla ice cream with a green crème de menthe sauce would fit in nicely. Bakery, market or homemade cookies complete the meal.

You might want to make small copies of *"When Irish Eyes are Smiling,"* and pass them to your guests at dessert time. Encourage them to sing along as you toast to the Irish with sparkling champagne:

> *When Irish eyes are smiling*
> *Sure 'tis like a morn in spring.*
> *In the lilt of Irish laughter*
> *You can hear the angels sing.*
> *When Irish hearts are happy*
> *All the world seems bright and gay,*
> *And when Irish eyes are smiling,*
> *Sure and they'll steal your heart away.*

Easter Party

Easter brings to mind visions of pink-eared bunnies, fluffy yellow chicks, and colored eggs nested in baskets of Easter grass – candy eggs, wooden eggs, plastic eggs, hard-boiled eggs, dyed or painted eggs, eggs in potted plants and centerpieces, and eggs as favors. Color hard-boiled eggs using packaged dye or food coloring, or just leave them white. Then, with your eggs as your "canvas," collect fabric, stick-ons, thin ribbons, tiny buttons, sequins, sprinkles and rickrack for use in trimming them.

When you don't plan on using edible eggs for decorations, poke a needle hole in each end of fresh eggs and slowly blow out the contents, which can be saved for scrambling at a later time. Spray paint the empty whole shells, or paint designs on them using acrylic paints.

Or, again using a needle, make a series of small holes around the diameter of fresh eggs, and with a sharp knife, carefully cut apart the two halves. ***Do not try to save the insides since they will have been contaminated with bits of shell.***

The empty half shells can be painted and filled with Easter scenes, tiny candy Easter eggs, or tiny flowers. If the edges of the shells are too rough, cover them with Easter "grass," leaves from small plants, fresh parsley or watercress. These eggshell "vases" are especially charming when filled with violas (tiny pansies) or lacy primulas. Use small pieces of water-saturated florist oasis to hold the flowers and keep them fresh. Whether you use hollowed out whole egg shells or half shells for your decorations, bear in mind that they will keep from year to year, so the effort spent decorating them will reap dividends in years to come.

Egg cups of all kinds are ideal bases for your decorated eggs, but there are also a variety of other holders (plastic, metal and terra cotta) which are generally available in party and specialty stores. Interesting bases can be found in the plumbing department of hardware stores – for example, flanges, large diameter nuts and pipe couplings. The plastic items can be spray painted more successfully than the rougher metal parts (see photograph on page 98).

White chocolate truffles rolled in colored sugar and placed in tiny baskets look like birds' eggs in a nest and make unique table favors. Many small commercial food containers can be decorated attractively in a variety of ways, filled with candy, and used as favors. For example, spray small egg cartons and fill them with decorated eggs, or cookies shaped to fit, or chocolate truffles – or a combination of all three.

When my children were still in playpens and eating baby food, I made favors for an Easter party using the empty baby food jars. Stripped of their labels and thoroughly washed, I sprayed both the lids and the jars white, painted bunny faces on the jars, and made the caps into Easter "bonnets" for the ladies and "top hats" for the men. These "jar hats" are pictured on pages 97 and 98; a templet for making the jar hats follows on the next page.

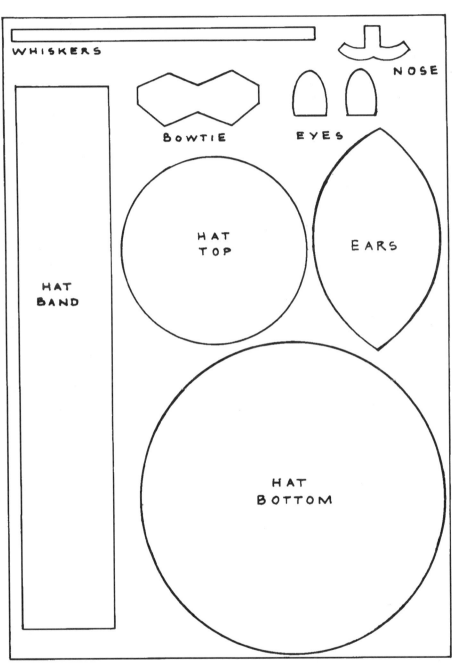

Templet (pattern) for making "jar hats"

This a fun project, but needs to be started several weeks in advance! Gather together colored paper, ribbons, laces, tiny artificial flowers (found in floral supply stores or miniature shops), as you run across them. Keep these materials, including the jars you have saved, in a box until you are ready to start your project. Once completed, fill your "bunnies" with Easter candies or nuts.

For a great way to entertain guests of all ages, ask each guest to bring an Easter egg which he or she has decorated, giving prizes for the most elaborate, the funniest, the most beautiful, etc.

Or you might hide your own decorated hard-boiled eggs, and perhaps some plastic eggs with some change inside, in your yard (or inside the house if the weather is inclement) for your guests to find. Give each person a bag or basket to put their findings in and to take home with them. Have prizes for the most eggs or money found.

For prizes, shop for decorated eggs, books on eggs, egg timers, egg cups, bunny or chick cookie cutters, movie videos ("*Easter Parade*"), stickers, candy, etc.

In most parts of the world, lamb is traditional for the Easter feast, although occasionally I have served baked ham or a ham loaf. In England, however, the traditional Easter meal is roast beef with Yorkshire pudding, with a creamy trifle for dessert. Once I put on a Greek Easter dinner and served moussaka made with ground lamb, green salad with feta cheese and Greek Easter bread. For dessert, I served baklava and Ouzo (see Greek Party Theme, page 149).

Kentucky Derby Day ("The Run for the Roses") Party

This is another perfect time to have your garden party. On the first Saturday in May the weather is generally warm and lovely and spring flowers are at their best.

Cocktail party fare, such as sliced ham, turkey and beef, provide the perfect buffet. Accompany them with various breads, crackers and cheeses, cold pasta or fruit salads, and dishes of various mustards, mayonnaise, and dressings.

Cheese slices may be cut into derby hat or horse shapes using cookie cutters. You can have the delicatessen slice the cheese for you first (freeze and save any leftover pieces to grate or melt for future use). Cap deviled eggs with miniature roses or tiny trumpet horns which can be found in toy or party supply stores and in many other stores around Christmas.

Line derby hats, which can be purchased at a party store, with heavy plastic "rounds," similar to those used by florists, and fill with flowers, preferably roses. Use replicas of horses, riding crops, saddles, horseshoes, and racing forms in your decorations.

Several television sets placed around the house will allow your guests easy viewing. You might want to ask a guest to be the announcer and to devise your own pool or other betting system, awarding the money wagered to the winner(s).

Mint juleps are the traditional drink for this occasion. They are quite smooth and very tasty, but also very potent, and they go down fast – *so have lots of coffee available.*

My father used to make truly marvelous juleps. He would start them the day before the party by crushing several sprigs of fresh mint in a large mixing bowl with a pestle, adding bourbon, and then allowing the mixture to steep overnight.

Tall glasses were placed in the freezer hours before serving time; then removed, nicely frosted, and filled with crushed ice. They were filled with the "steeped" bourbon (a judicious amount of water may be added depending on the potency desired) and topped off with a shot glass of white crème de menthe. Lastly, a fresh sprig of mint was tucked into the glass for a flourish.

Those juleps were not easily forgotten!

Mother's Day Party

Consider hosting a tea (see Teas, page 61) for your mother. Invite a few of her very best friends and include several of your close friends, and their mothers as well. Give each mother a small corsage that you have made yourself or ordered through your local florist or "flower person."

Like Father's Day, this occasion calls for a gathering of family members and close friends for a special luncheon or dinner, formal or informal, that mother does not have to cook.

Father's Day Party

This is the kind of day to be spent with family and close friends. It should be a relaxing time for all; the dress and food should be informal and casual.

It's a perfect time to have a barbecue, but ask someone else to do the honors so that your "king-for-the-day" can be free of any culinary responsibilities. Straw place mats and napkins tied with raffia go well with the informality of this party theme.

At dessert time, I like to crown all fathers present. The crowns can be purchased at any party goods store and many stationery stores. You (or your children) can also make your own.

For favors, you might purchase tiny screwdrivers, attaching place cards to them with thin ribbon or raffia. Give them to both the men and the ladies, who might find them very handy in the kitchen.

One year I sprayed the lids of little jam jars I had saved, and glued various sized nuts and bolts to them. I filled the ladies' jars with thumbtacks, pins and paper clips; the men's with assorted screws, nuts, bolts and washers. I tied the place cards around the base of the lids.

For another Fathers' Day favor, I visited my local floral supply store and picked up some small Shaker-type boxes, which I sprayed with lacquer. I glued miniature cowboy hats with feathers to the tops, and from the fabric store, I purchased thin gold "rope" which I glued to the base of the lid. Then I filled the boxes with nuts and candy. These are also perfect favors for a western party. See photograph of decorated boxes on page 97.

Memorial Day/July Fourth/Labor Day Party

Now we're getting into the serious barbecue season!

It is also a good time to have a garden party or a picnic. The weather is likely to be very warm; shorts and sundresses are clearly the appropriate attire for the day. Stores will display their red, white and blue merchandise weeks in advance, which provides ample time for planning and shopping for these parties.

Whatever you decide to barbecue (hamburgers, chicken, fish, or a roast), make dessert the "star" of your dinner. Tie a red, white and blue ribbon around the base of a frosted layer cake. Stick miniature flags in cookies and cookie bars.

Using your favorite recipe, bake a cake or pie; spread it with a thin layer of whipping cream, white frosting or vanilla ice cream, and then make an American flag design using blueberries for the stars and strawberries for the stripes.

For favors, place a flat gumdrop in a white ramekin (custard-type dish) and stick a small American flag in the middle, then fill it with red, white and blue jelly beans. Interesting containers can be filled with jelly beans such as the one shown in the photograph on page 87 which illustrates a place setting for a patriotic theme party.

Another idea for favors: place red, white or blue candles in ramekins, or on miniature plates or dishes. Use red candles with blue and white ware which can be found in discount stores and some Chinese import stores, or mix and match with what you have or can borrow.

Play your best marching music on the stereo or CD player!

Halloween Party

Concentrate on the autumn colors that complement your Halloween theme, particularly orange, yellow and black.

Group pumpkins of various sizes near the front door. Cut and decorate the largest one to light with a candle when it's dark. Fill some of the smaller ones with hot water and drop in chunks of dry ice to make a mist, but wait until just before your guests start to arrive or the dry ice will evaporate before anyone can see the clever effect you have created.

Cut the top off a pumpkin and remove the seeds and "string," then wash it out and use it as a centerpiece "vase." Fill it with multicolored chrysanthemums. I have found that a teaspoon of vodka or Clorox added to the water will keep the flowers perked up and fresh for several days.

If it appeals to you, spray some fall leaves black and tuck them in the floral arrangement, or if you can successfully protect (cover) the blossoms, spray the leaves and stems of the flowers black before assembling your arrangement. Fill mini pumpkins with tiny bouquets or use them to hold votive candles.

Pumpkins may determine your menu from appetizer to dessert. Small ones, emptied and cleaned, can be used to hold cheese spreads, carrot sticks, pumpkin soup or bisque, and orange ices; larger ones can be used as serving dishes for steaming stews (see Irish Party Theme, page 167) and spicy chilis or curries. You might want to be imaginative and "color" cooked pasta or rice using grated orange peel. Pumpkin purée can be used to make muffins, cookies, cheesecakes, puddings and, of course, pies.

For favors, fill "trick or treat" bags with candy, "creepy crawlers" or paperback mysteries – and hang them on the back of each guest's chair or pass them out at the door as your guests depart. For entertainment, find a tarot card reader (if your party is relatively small), or rent a scary movie. On your CD player or stereo, play spooky music, which is available at most music stores at Halloween time.

Many fabric stores carry a selection of Halloween colors and prints for those of you who might want to make your own place mats, cloths and napkins.

A note to the thrifty: after Halloween is over, spray your uncut pumpkins gold and save them in a cool place for use later when decorating for holiday parties – they look stunning nestled amongst green plants and shrubbery.

Christmas Parties

Of all the holidays throughout the year, Christmas seems to be the most favorite one of all. It gives us a chance to entertain in a variety of ways over a period of several weeks. It is the time for giving parties and for going to parties.

I get into gear just after Thanksgiving, when it is time to begin planning and organizing our yuletide entertainment, and reviewing menus to see which foods can be prepared ahead and frozen. I start baking cookies, cakes and Christmas breads for the family to enjoy and for gifts to give to friends and neighbors. The spicy aroma permeating the house reminds everyone in the household of home, family and friends as well as our most favorite traditions.

There is always a child within us, and this is the time of year to "play." With joy and eagerness we can bring forth dolls and teddy bears to set by the hearth or under the tree; fill tables, mantles and all sorts of empty places with miniature toys and gingerbread men.

This is the time for children and grown-ups to celebrate and play as one; a time to share in shopping, wrapping presents, and decorating cookies and Christmas trees. Let the children wrap packages in plain paper and then, with crayons or colored ink pens, decorate them with their personalized drawings and special messages. Later, they can be tied with colorful fabric ribbons.

You might wish to put small trees in several rooms and decorate them according to the color scheme and usage of the room. Let the children have the responsibility and excitement of decorating their own tree in their own bedroom.

For the kitchen, drape the tree with strings of popcorn, cranberries or gumdrops, and add cookie cutters and "cookies" made from *non-edible bread dough* as ornaments. To make bread dough, mix 4 cups unsifted flour, 2 cups salt and 2 cups cold water, and knead until the consistency of molding clay. Cut into shapes, making a hole for hanging if desired. Bake in preheated 300° oven for 40-45 minutes. After cooling, paint with acrylics; after drying, spray with lacquer.

If you want to hang *edible* home baked cookies from a tree to be served at a tea, luncheon or children's party, wait until the last minute to hang them because they may soften and fall off.

Get your Christmas tree and set up decorations early in December. Tree lots usually open by the first of December, and you want to get the most enjoyment, and entertaining potential, out of your holiday decorations.

When you get your tree home, cut at least two inches off the end of the trunk and place the tree in a bucket of water, with a shot or two of vodka added to it, for about two days before you place it in a water-filled stand. If you check the tree every three or four days to make certain that there is enough water to cover the end of the trunk, it should stay green for four to six weeks – although it will become dry and brittle.

Some of the prettiest holiday centerpieces are the simplest to do. A mixture of greens provides a perfect base for a display of cranberries, nuts, pine cones, grapes (sugared or plain) and crab apples. To sugar grapes, dip them in beaten egg whites, shake off the excess and dip them in granulated sugar; set on wax paper to dry.

Votives nestled in the various boughs of green can provide ample illumination. The abundant use of votives, on end tables, mantles, bookshelves, amongst silver tea services, on silver trays – everywhere and anywhere – makes an enchanting atmosphere.

For party favors, cover small boxes with Christmas fabric and fill them with tiny gingerbread men as shown in the picture on page 95. Or buy plain colored ornaments and decorate them yourself – by painting them if you are artistically inclined – or by gluing on glitter, ribbon and wood or plastic miniatures. If you prefer, look for ready made ornaments that harmonize with your guests' life styles, tastes or occupations. Tie place cards to the ornaments using a thin ribbon, or tie them to the napkins.

Small Christmas stockings that you can make yourself, or buy at specialty shops, are also fun "place cards" and favors. Fill them with small useful gifts obtained from the market, hardware, stationery or bath stores, or fill them with candy, cookies, nuts or small jars of jam. Hang them on the backs of the guests' chairs. Tie place cards to the stockings or to the end of candy canes peeking from their tops.

If you are going to make your own stockings, make a templet out of cardboard and trace the outline onto a double piece of red or green felt, then cut along the tracing. At the top of each piece, sew or glue a cuff cut from some holiday fabric. Make a "hanger" out of the same fabric or the felt, whichever is stronger. Sew or glue the two stocking halves together, then attach the hanger.

Christmas Eve or Christmas night dinner is the most traditional one for many of us, and we look forward to the Christmas turkey, chicken or goose. Others may feast on succulent ham or serve the very British roast beef with Yorkshire pudding (see English Party Theme, page 187).

Our family tradition is to serve a roast turkey with stuffing, mashed potatoes, gravy, dried corn casserole (a Pennsylvania Dutch favorite of my father's), creamed peas and onions, and homemade cranberry sauce. For a festive finale, we choose between a steamed chocolate pudding served with vanilla sauce and bedecked with small candy canes or a persimmon pudding served with brandied hard sauce and surrounded by *non-edible* holly leaves.

If you celebrate Christmas with dinner on Christmas Eve, hide a shelled almond in the dessert. This Old World custom gives the one who finds the almond the honor of opening the first Christmas present when that time arrives.

You might wish to be a bit unusual in your invitations by tying an international theme into your Christmas party. Listed below are some foreign translations of "Merry Christmas," which you might incorporate into your invitations:

Sweden: *Glad Jul*
France: *Joyeux Noël*
Spain/Mexico: *Feliz Navidad*
Italy: *Buon Natale*
Greece: *Kele Kristougene or Kala Kristougena*

The list of holiday parties is endless. You can choose from luncheons or dinners, either buffet or sit-down, or cocktail parties, any of which can be as casually informal or as elegantly formal as you wish. A few suggestions for a variety of holiday parties follow – personalize them with additions and embellishments which reflect your own style and approach:

Cocktail and tree trimming party

This is a great idea for an easy and informal affair to be given by younger couples. Start the party around eight in the evening and serve simmering spiced cider, a wassail bowl, or a frothy cold eggnog (see Menu Suggestions for Buffet and Cocktail Parties, page 121).

The food needn't be fancy nor fussy; it can be as simple as popcorn and pretzels, or an assortment of colorful cookies and cookie bars. Play your Christmas tapes or CDs, and encourage your guests to sing along while everyone helps in trimming the tree.

For something different, ask your guests to bring an ornament appropriate for a small tree which would be trimmed during the party and later taken to a housebound or less fortunate family. Send everyone home with a loaf of homemade bread, a bottle of your herbed vinegar, or a box of chocolate truffles which you can make or purchase. Tie the gift with red and green ribbon and attach a small jingle bell.

Informal potluck dinner (see page 42)

You might choose a buffet dinner for this party. Gather your guests together and stroll around the neighborhood caroling friends and neighbors. This works especially well either between dinner and dessert or after the meal is finished, when you return for a cup of hot chocolate, coffee or expresso.

Cocktail or dinner party with a caroling group

Professional or semiprofessional caroling groups are often available from your local church or school. They may also be listed in your local newspaper or in the Yellow Pages under *Entertainment* or *Singing*. Many such groups perform in period costumes, such as the style of Dickens's London.

Have the carolers arrive during a break in the party activities so all of your guests will be able to enjoy the entertainment. Provide the words of the carols and, by prearrangement with the performers, toward the end of the performance encourage your guests to sing along.

Formal, sit-down English dinner (see page 187)

Following dinner, gather your guests in the living room with a crackling fire as the backdrop, and have a guest who feels comfortable read Dickens's Christmas Carol.

Family gathering, formal or informal

Purchase or make Christmas ornaments for each family member, appropriately labeled with their names, and hide them in various places on your Christmas tree. During the predinner cocktail period, ask your guests to find their ornaments.

Christmas bridal luncheon and shower

Suggest the gifts your guests bring for the bride-to-be reflect the Christmas season, such as special ornaments, candles, china with a Christmas motif, wrapping paper, matches, tins, cookbooks, books of Christmas stories, angels, Santas, etc.

For favors, tie an ornament to each napkin or fill lacy handkerchiefs with potpourri or tiny gifts of soap, perfumes or sachets. Using holiday ribbon, tie a place card to each napkin. If you are handy with a needle, you can make your own handkerchiefs out of Christmas fabrics.

Guests bring gifts for "him "or "her" party

The object is to involve your guests in the gift giving spirit of the season. Each gift should be marked whether it is "for him" or "for her." At an appropriate moment, probably before the meal, have someone dressed as Santa distribute the gifts at random.

Feliz Navidad (Mexican Christmas party)

This type of party is made very festive with the use of Mexican sombreros and piñatas, possibly a mariachi band, and delicious Mexican Christmas breads and cakes (see Mexican Party Theme, page 161).

Post-Christmas leftovers party

Most people have substantial amounts of food left over from Christmas dinner and other parties given during the holidays. What could be more enjoyable than sharing delicious leftovers by a warm and cozy fire with family and good friends.

Twelfth-night (January 6th) party

This is a wonderful opportunity to give one last party before you take down your Christmas finery and decorations, and put them away for another year. For dessert, serve a Twelfth-night cake in which an almond or foil-wrapped coin has been placed before baking. Crown the guest who finds the hidden good luck piece in his or her slice of cake. Paper crowns can be purchased at party stores.

There are many variations of recipes for Twelfth-night cake. Some are made with a puff pastry crust, others with a yeast dough. However, a simple spicy, rich pound cake, topped with glacéed fruit will do.

Christmas bridge party

I would like to share with you a tradition I started many years ago.

Each year I host a bridge luncheon for twelve of my very good friends, all of whom are like family to me. I schedule the party for a day in early December after we have our Christmas decorations up, but before the holiday rush is in full force. We start at eleven and play bridge until lunch, which I serve about one. After lunch, we continue our bridge games until someone has to leave.

Bridge is not an essential part of the party. You could start a bit later, around noon or so, but keep the number of guests small or the party will lose its warm, intimate appeal. Give each of your guests a small gift as they leave.

If you do decide to play bridge, set up two or three tables, which do not all have to be in the same room. Although you need guests in multiples of four, do not include yourself in the count in case someone cancels the morning of the party. Also, being an extra person will allow you to pamper your guests and to get the luncheon on without interruptions.

Make a substitute list in advance and have it available, because most likely it will be needed to keep your numbers correct for bridge.

Plan a menu that can be put on the table fairly quickly. You will thank yourself many times if you organize and cook well ahead of the party date.

I set up the beverages on a long buffet chest with a smaller table next to it for coffee. The buffet lunch is served from the dining room table and the desserts from a smaller table nearby. Depending on your needs and space, you may want to set up card tables as "food stations," or you may wish to be casual and serve in your kitchen.

Decorate your tables and serving areas with Christmas tree boughs, holly, ornaments and whatever else will create a festive mood and put your guests in the holiday spirit.

The beverages I provide include wine, Bloody Marys, iced tea, soft drinks and mineral water. On the coffee table, I have coffee, a pitcher of cream (or milk) and another of brandy. Sometimes I serve a dish of whipped cream. I also include brown sugar cubes and decorated white sugar cubes (available in specialty stores) and rock sugar candy if I can find it.

The luncheon menu varies from year to year. I start thinking about various possibilities two to three months before the party. I use a large manila envelope in which I keep notes, recipes, magazine articles and pictures of Christmas party ideas I have been collecting over the years. The choices range from salads and quiches, to rolls, muffins and breads. I serve either a green salad with a quiche, or if the salad is the main dish, I choose a single hearty salad or two lighter ones, molded or tossed, and arranged on a platter.

Dessert always remains the same. I serve four kinds of miniature tarts: one is filled with mincemeat topped with hard sauce and decorated with red and green sprinkles; another is filled with lemon curd topped with whipped cream and a chocolate candy leaf; the third is filled with chocolate mousse topped with whipped cream and a red raspberry or a white chocolate leaf; and the fourth is filled with a custard pudding topped with slices of fresh fruit.

All of these tarts can be made well in advance and frozen. If you have any pumpkin or pecan pie filling left over from Thanksgiving, use it to fill the premade tarts and freeze them.

Lunch is served buffet-style and eaten at the bridge tables. At each guest's place are snacks to be nibbled on while playing bridge with enough left to be taken home afterwards.

I vary the containers for the snacks depending on what I find during shopping trips; sometimes, I might buy them months in advance. I have used colorful metal tins and paper boxes, glass jars or little baskets decorated with colorful Christmas ribbon.

I have decorated my own tins and boxes; I have also bought them already decorated. The containers are always filled with a variety of mixed nuts, which I have preroasted in oil and salted (see Buffet and Cocktail Parties, page 129) and then frozen until needed.

Each guest contributes $2.00 towards a prize (it can be less, or you can generously supply the entire amount), which is presented to the high scoring winner of the day. The player with the lowest score gets a small gift for being a good sport. Occasionally, I make a basket of little prizes for the players who bid and make small or grand slams. This adds to the excitement!

I have always given each guest a small gift to take home. When I first started this tradition, my children were young and our budget was tight, so I made my gifts. I decorated candles and ornaments with ribbon and "jewels." I made ornaments from plastic movie reels (on which developed film was returned from processing) by cutting them into spokes, spray painting them and decorating them with Christmas figures, jewels, ribbons, etc.

I filled baskets with cookies, breads or plants, and attached Christmas ribbons. Sometimes, I tried to personalize the favors to complement the taste and color preferences of each guest; or I filled stockings and tote bags with a variety of little gifts: teas, jams, Christmas memo pads, pencils, soaps, and so forth.

One year, I planned a "Twelve Days of Christmas" party theme. Each gift corresponded to a "day of Christmas," and after everyone had opened their gifts, we sang the entire song with each guest responsible for the stanza relating to her day.

Use your own imagination when selecting gifts for this theme party. You might consider buying a small pear tree from the local nursery and a facsimile of a partridge from a floral supply store, as I did. As a memory jogger, those twelve days are:

First: a partridge in a pear tree
Second: two turtle doves
Third: three French horns
Fourth: four calling birds
Fifth: five golden rings
Sixth: six geese a-laying
Seventh: seven swans a-swimming
Eighth: eight maids a-milking
Ninth: nine drummers drumming
Tenth: ten pipers piping
Eleventh: eleven ladies dancing
Twelfth: twelve Lords a-leaping

Other favors or gifts might include magazine subscriptions, picture frames, planted baskets, something special picked up while traveling, or boxes of all shapes, sizes and colors. Or bake and decorate your favorite cakes, cookies or breads and place them in baskets or tins.

One year I filled tall Italian glass bottles with homemade sherry wine vinegar. I tied the bottles with ribbon and raffia, borrowed a small antique trunk, filled it with greens and boughs, and put it on the hearth with bottles inside. Another year I hired a Santa to pass out the gifts.

Instead of a luncheon, you might apply the "Twelve Days of Christmas" theme to a dinner party. Print the words of the song on a piece of Christmas note paper, leaving room at the top for the guest's name. Assign a number to each guest and mark it inside the song sheet.

Following dessert, have the host lead the group in song. Pass out gifts to match the numbered "day" as that day comes up in the song. Or, if you prefer, they can be numbered for the day, placed under the tree and collected by the guests, in sequence, after dinner while dessert and coffee are being served in the living room. Merry Christmas!

FOODS AND FOOD PRESENTATIONS

There is nothing that whets the appetite more than entering a home filled with the intoxicating aromas of wine and garlic simmering in a stew, freshly baked bread and rolls, homemade spicy gingerbread and freshly brewed coffee!

Sitting down to a nicely prepared meal should be a pleasant and enjoyable experience. Whether it be soup and muffins served by the fire, hot dogs and hamburgers sizzling on the barbecue, or a formal affair by candlelight in the dining room, you can still make your meal as simple or elegant as you wish depending on your budget, your taste, and the time you have to devote to the details.

Good meals and good parties do not have to be complicated, fussy and time-consuming affairs, especially if you are new at the game. You do, however, want your food to be visually tempting. As you plan your menu, vary both the color and texture of the dishes served. For example, you would not want to have two creamed dishes on the same plate.

Plan ahead!

Organize your food into groups. Starting with the entrée, select your appetizers, salads, vegetables, breads and desserts. Allow yourself several choices, then coordinate your selections into a balanced meal. Keep a market list handy and add to it as you go along, reviewing it before you do your final shopping.

For last minute, unannounced or drop in company, keep a well stocked pantry and freezer. If you find yourself doing a lot of entertaining, and if your budget allows, consider adding a second refrigerator and/or freezer. This might sound like an extravagance, but you will fill it quickly, particularly if baking is a favorite pastime. Even your husband will later agree that it was a cost-effective expenditure.

We are used to serving salads as a first course or along with the main course. An alternative, which is the European approach, is to serve the salad between the entrée and dessert courses.

Instead of bread or rolls, try miniature muffins served in silver or wicker baskets, or for garden parties, placed in napkin-lined terra cotta pots. There are many wonderful muffin books available to choose from. Keep in mind that etiquette guru Miss Manners says that bread should never be served at formal dinners – it is acceptable for casual affairs, luncheons and informal dinners, *but not formal dinners.*

Instead of potatoes, pasta or rice, you might want to serve baked quesadillas made of flour tortillas with one or two grated cheeses, and a combination of chopped tomatoes, onions, corn and green chilies, according to your taste. For a southwestern flavor, season them with a selection of spices such as chili powder, cumin, etc.

Since either red or white wine is now acceptable with any entrée, you might wish to serve a choice of both wines with dinner. This way everyone's taste is satisfied. For more formal occasions, consider a selection of liqueurs with coffee after dessert.

Since there are always a few basic things which are forgotten before any dinner party, consider making a check list for last minute review. Prominent on such a list should be:

Don't forget the salt and pepper!
Plug in the coffee maker!
Fill the water glasses with ice and water!
Pour the wine!
Light the candles!

After a wonderful dinner you might wish to move your guests into the living room for dessert, coffee and liqueur.

Do It Ahead

As you go about collecting recipes from books, magazines and friends, be sure to separate them into separate categories. Keep them in recipe boxes, manila envelopes or folders. Label them as follows, or whatever is easy for you:

- appetizers
- meats (beef, pork, lamb, etc.)
- poultry (chicken, turkey, etc.)
- fowl (duck, quail, etc.)
- seafoods
- stews, casseroles and pizzas
- cheese and egg dishes
- vegetables (including potatoes, rice, pasta)
- soups and sandwiches
- breads and muffins
- salads and dressings
- cookies, cakes and pies
- sauces and marinades
- pickles, jams and jellies
- foreign dishes

Study each recipe carefully before you start your food preparation. If you hurry, you might mix the ingredients improperly or add them in the wrong sequence, which could significantly alter the outcome of your dish.

Rinse your mixing bowls, pans and utensils as you go along, so they don't accumulate and become an overwhelming mountain.

Several days prior to the meal preparation, slice, mince, grate, dice and chop vegetables, nuts and cheese. Put the vegetables in a dish, cover with water, and place in the refrigerator to keep them fresh and crisp. Seal nuts and cheese in individual plastic bags and refrigerate. Put chopped parsley or chopped green onions in glass jars with tight fitting lids to better preserve them and contain their pungent aromas.

On the day of the party, wrap premeasured salad greens in damp dish towels to keep them crispy until you are ready to use them. Prepare extra amounts of some of the ingredients to keep on hand for last minute needs at a later date, such as spur-of-the-moment cooking, for salads or for topping breads or casseroles. Leftover chopped nuts and grated cheese can be frozen and saved for later use. Carrots can also be grated ahead and frozen for future use in salads or sautéed for a vegetable course.

If a friend gives you a bag of lemons or limes, first grate the rind and then squeeze the juice. Store in tightly closed jars in the refrigerator or freezer; you can freeze the juice in ice cube trays and use the individual cubes as needed.

When baking, mix the dry ingredients a day or two ahead of time. Once bread, cookie or pie dough has been made, it can be put in plastic bags and kept frozen until needed. Place forming and baking instructions with each bag of dough (or dry ingredients) to make sure you have the right ones when you get back to them.

For yeast doughs, gradually bring the dough to room temperature and let the dough rise as the instructions call for. After baking muffins and rolls, you might wish to butter them before freezing.

If you are serving ice cream or sherbet for dessert, soften it slightly, make your scoops and place them in individual dishes, muffin tins or storage containers, then return them to the freezer until ready to use.

Pie and tartlet shells can be made ahead of time and frozen until ready to fill. Depending on the type of filling, some pies can be frozen in their entirety until needed.

If you can't find a cookie cutter in the shape you want, make you own. Draw your pattern on a piece of heavy cardboard, cut it out, place it on the cookie dough and cut around it with a knife to form your cookie.

Save plastic squeeze containers. They can be used to drizzle chocolate on cakes and cookies, or for making patterns with raspberry sauce or *crème anglaise* to decorate the plates on which you serve cake slices.

Don't forget to think ahead. Use timesaving methods, as they will provide extra time for you on the day of your party; you will be more relaxed and better able to enjoy yourself and your guests.

For future reference, keep a notebook of what foods you served at each of your parties, and who attended them. This will help you avoid serving the same entrée or hors d'oeuvres at a second party attended by the same guests.

To keep your vegetarian friends happy, you might make a note to serve additional vegetables when you entertain them. It would also be helpful to note any particular likes or dislikes your guests may have, and whether they are allergic to any specific foods or spices.

My husband likes to barbecue lamb chops lathered with butter and dry mustard to give them a nice crust. One evening, as newlyweds, we invited one of his old friends over for barbecued lamb chops – only to discover during dinner, and much to our horror, that he was extremely allergic to mustard. That started my personal entertaining notebook!

Special Enhancements

Giving a little extra time to food presentation, the "special effects" of entertaining, is well worth the effort.

Making food pretty as well as tasty will please your guests and let them know you care about them. There are ways of decorating and garnishing with food and flowers, there are ways of filling pots, buckets and baskets with tempting foods, and all of these are fun to do and lovely to look at. They are not complicated nor difficult, and generally, may be done ahead of time.

I'll provide you with some starters and leave the rest up to you. Keep your eyes open when dining out; look for suggestions in books and magazines.

Food "Bowls" and Garnishes

Small *pineapples*, *cantaloupes* and *papaya* are sensational when filled with chicken or seafood salad, ice cream or sherbets. Garnish them with chopped or slivered nuts, parsley or mint. Decorate with edible flowers (see edible flowers, page 109) or paper parasols.

Fill *orange* shells with cranberry sauce, sweet potato soufflé or sherbets; *pear* halves with mint jelly; *peach* halves with chutney; *tomatoes* with tartar sauce; *avocados* with salsa, chilled gazpacho, jellied (chilled) consommé or vinaigrette sauce.

Use *lemon* shells as individual "bowls" for tartar sauce, cocktail sauce or mint jelly. Large *lemons*, *limes* and *oranges* make perfect "ramekins" for sorbets and sherbets to be served with dinner or with hearty salads. Hollowed out green, red and yellow *peppers* and red or green *cabbages* make colorful containers for dips.

Small round loaves of *French bread* "bowls" are festive when filled with thick soups, hot dips and stews (see page 170). *Pumpkins* and *squashes* also make wonderful receptacles for soups and stews.

Try setting bowls of soup or salad inside wreaths of natural herbs or flowers. Cut notches in thick pieces of *carrots* so they look like flowers; cut *cheeses* into shapes of flowers or stars.

Styrofoam

Styrofoam can be purchased or cut into any shape you want. Place a cone "tree" on a silver or china pedestal base; "dress" it with sprigs of parsley attached with hair pins and shrimp secured with toothpicks. Since Styrofoam cones tend to be tippy, hollow out a three to four inch hole in the bottom and pack with pie weights,

For a wreath effect, cover a round shape with parsley, watercress or curly lettuce secured with hairpins; place a candle or a small dish of dip or sauce in the center, and using toothpicks, "plant" the rest with vegetables, shrimp or cheeses.

Sandwich Art

Serve three or four small sandwiches as an accompaniment to a fruit, chicken, seafood or vegetable salad.

Cut partially frozen bread into several different shapes, such as hearts, stars, diamonds, flowers or circles, and alternate white and wheat bread for each sandwich.

If you have cutters which come in various sizes, cut a smaller shape in the center of the top piece of bread so the filling peeks through. Fruit breads and brown breads can be cut into shapes and spread with flavored butter or cream cheese.

Fillings for your sandwiches will depend upon the kind of salad you are serving. Besides cream cheese and herbed cheese, try sliced chicken, deviled ham, deviled egg, jelly with cream cheese (or cream cheese mixed with orange marmalade, pineapple or berry preserves), thinly sliced roast beef with horseradish, and thinly sliced cucumbers

with chive mayonnaise. My husband insisted that I add his favorite –
sliced pimiento-stuffed green olives on cream cheese.

The Swedes serve open-faced sandwiches which can be layered with
beef, shrimp, cucumbers or avocado, fresh dill, carrot curls, chopped
egg, capers, etc. Garnish with edible flowers (see edible flowers, page
109).

Plant toothpicks festooned with miniature flags, name tags, flowers,
beads or plastic miniatures in each sandwich. Decorative toothpicks
are available at most markets as well as liquor and party stores.

For Halloween, cut dark pumpernickel bread into bats, cats and
witches. Spread them with creamy yellow cheese or orange-tinted
cream cheese.

A Way With Butter

Slice pats of butter, and using tiny cookie cutters, cut them into
flowers, hearts, stars, etc. Fill decorative plastic molds (see Catalogs –
Maid of Scandinavia, page 34) with butter, freeze, then remove from
the mold.

There are wonderful plastic molds available to use for holiday or
theme parties. It's more fun to see a butter bunny standing on the
butter plate than a plain yellow square.

Make herbed butter, cut into shapes and serve on baked potatoes and
steaks. For an added flair, garnish with small edible flowers as
illustrated on page 91.

Fun With Flower Pots

For garden and patio parties, flower pots of all sizes may be filled with
an assortment of "dry" foods: peanuts, popcorn, pretzels, potato chips,
rolls, muffins, cookies and candies. Baskets also make attractive
containers for these foods.

A dessert that will delight every guest, and make your party a memorable one, consists of packing a scoop or two of your favorite ice cream into a foil-lined flower pot. Bake cookies in flower shapes (see templet on page 45). Paint wooden or bamboo skewers with green food coloring. Attach the cookies with white chocolate "glue" (see next page). For a finished look, add a white chocolate leaf before the glue hardens. Plant the "flower" in the ice cream and surround the base with dark chocolate sauce.

Dazzle at Dessert Time

While dining at Michelle's in Honolulu, a bowl of *strawberries* became a dramatic presentation. Dry ice had been placed in a silver stemmed compote, and a sturdy glass dish filled with luscious large strawberries was placed on top. When served, the "smoke" from the dry ice cascaded from around the lip of the compote making a unique and very pleasing effect.

Large strawberries, with the stem left on to form a handle, are delicious when dipped in melted dark or white chocolate, then chilled. Finish by drizzling those dipped in dark chocolate with melted white chocolate, and vice versa, chill until served.

To make after dinner mints more interesting, melt thin mints, either chocolate or pastels, and fill decorative molds (see Catalogs – Maid of Scandinavia, page 34). Refrigerate or freeze them until they are firm, then remove them from the molds. Cover with plastic wrap and keep them refrigerated until served. This can be done several weeks in advance of your party.

Another dazzling dessert I'll never forget was served to us on our honeymoon, again in Hawaii, at the Hana Maui Hotel. Velvety *papaya* halves, filled with coffee ice cream, were sprinkled with Cointreau and topped with clouds of whipped cream. For a very dramatic effect, sugar cubes soaked in lemon extract were placed on top of the whipped cream and ignited.

If you don't want to use *papaya*, improvise. For instance, you can fill small, hollowed out *pineapples* or *cantaloupes* with sherbet or ice cream – then top with lemon extract-soaked sugar cubes and ignite.

Or make a cake "hat." This is done by placing an iced cake in the center of a large round plate. The exposed portion of the plate becomes the brim of the hat. Using more icing or melted white and dark chocolate, "glue" a real ribbon around the base of the cake as the hatband. Attach a bow to the ribbon or decorate it with edible flowers and lace. If you wish, make small individual cake hats for each guest.

Instead of a hat, you might prefer a cake "basket," using melted white or dark chocolate for the handle. If you wish, you can bake and ice your cake ahead of time and freeze it. On the morning of the party, unthaw the cake and attach the handle. Give yourself plenty of time in case the handle breaks while you are placing it on the cake. In that case you will need time to repair it and for the chocolate glue to harden.

To form the handle, use a piece of wire or twisted foil and experiment with different sizes and shapes. Try them on the cake to determine which you like best, but do this before you ice the cake to avoid messing up the frosting. After deciding on the size and shape of the handle, draw it on a piece of wax paper, allowing an extra inch or so on the ends for that portion of the handle which goes into the cake.

Pour melted white or dark chocolate into a small plastic squeeze bottle (a mustard squeeze bottle with the tip cut off will do nicely, or bottles for this very purpose can be purchased from cake decorating stores). Insert a toothpick as a stopper, and place the bottle in a cup of hot water. This prevents the chocolate from hardening.

Drizzle the chocolate onto the wax paper in a crisscross fashion following the outline of the pattern. Place it in the refrigerator until it is firm. Repeat the process a second time, and again refrigerate until firm. Place another sheet of wax paper on top and turn it over. Carefully peel the handle off the wax paper and drizzle the second side as described above. This adds strength and gives a finished look to both sides. Refrigerate until ready for use. The handles may be made

in advance, covered, and kept in the refrigerator for up to two weeks. They can also be frozen.

You might even like to try making individual cake baskets or setting small handles into individual ice cream baskets. For a quick and easy alternative, fashion a handle from pipe cleaners and cover with ribbon.

How many of you remember "snowballs" for dessert at Christmas? Vanilla ice cream balls, rolled in coconut and topped with a red or green candle, a candy holly leaf or tiny candy cane. Served with hot chocolate sauce or crème de menthe, they were the highlight of the season.

Edible Flowers

Flowers contribute so much to every aspect of the dining experience. Many are edible, some people say delectable as well as decorative, but you must be careful to eat only the right ones (see below). *And if you are buying your flowers, be sure you determine that they are both edible **and** pesticide free!*

Although flowers look lovely in a salad, some people are a little nervous about eating them, even though they have been assured that they are edible.

The most fun comes from using them decoratively, where they may be eaten or removed. Consider a potpourri of tiny flowers sprinkled over the icing of a cake. Roses are very pretty used this way, *but the whole flower should not be eaten since the white portion at the base of the petal is bitter*. The rest of the petal, however, is quite tasty.

Primroses and lily of the valley can be toxic, and should be avoided, even for use as decoration.

Wash flowers gently and float them in a pan of water, then put them in a cool place or in the refrigerator. I have picked them the day before a party with fairly good results.

If you need a specific number of flowers to decorate deviled eggs, for example, make sure you pick (or buy) more than you need in order to allow for bruising or wilting.

Arrange single flowers or bouquets on platters of appetizers and meats.

Rosalind Creasy, author of *Cooking from the Garden*, lists the following flowers where **only the petals are edible:**

roses	chrysanthemums
calendulas	lavender

Also, according to Rosalind Creasy, the following flowers where the **whole flowers are edible:**

geraniums	violets
pinks	johnny-jumpups
pansies	violas
nasturtiums (a peppery, watercress flavor)	

Flowers of herbs are reportably tasty as well as being attractive garnishings for vegetable platters or pats of butter. The flowers of the following herbs **taste the same as the herbs:**

chives	sage
oregano	arrugula
thyme	fennel
basil	rosemary
borage (cucumber taste)	

More Special Touches

If you are planning to serve *champagne* with dessert, and have room in your freezer, your guests will enjoy the added touch of drinking from chilled, frosted glasses.

Stolichnaya in an ice jacket is very effective as part of your appetizer buffet. Locate it next to caviar, melba toast and condiments (chopped onions and separately chopped whites and yolks of hard-boiled eggs).

An eye-catching finale to your cocktail buffet dinner is a bottle of *Stolichnaya* (Russian Vodka) encased in a floral jacket of ice (see illustration on page 91). Presented along with dessert, this is especially good with strawberries dipped in chocolate.

To make the ice jacket, place a bottle of Stolichnaya in a milk carton half-filled with water, add any small colorful flowers (they do not have to be edible), gently pressing them down into the water, then freeze. Then add more water and flowers, and freeze again, continuing the process until the frozen jacket reaches the neck of the bottle. Peel off the milk carton and keep frozen until ready to serve – then put it on a chilled, lipped and footed tray on the buffet along with your liqueur glasses.

When serving *coffee*, try substituting whipped cream for regular cream. For another special touch, serve brandy alongside in a pretty silver, glass or china pitcher. You will also delight your guests by serving hand decorated sugar cubes, brown sugar cubes or rock sugar candy stirrers.

For chocolate lovers, serve chocolate mint sticks, chocolate curls, shaved chocolate or spoons dipped in melted chocolate and hardened in the refrigerator. Include a small dish of orange peel to complement the chocolate or to add a unique flavor to the coffee.

Cinnamon sticks also enhance the flavor of the coffee.

For a tasty and eye appealing garnish for *soups*, cut out shapes from *puff pastry* (found in the freezer section of your market) and bake according to the package instructions. Just before serving, float on top of the soup.

Additionally, puff pastry cutouts make great toppings for simmering stews and casseroles.

Instead of covering *pies* with traditional lattices or blankets of crust, cut shapes out of piecrust dough with cookie cutters, paint them with a wash of egg yolk and water, and bake until they are golden brown. After the pie has been baked, place the cutouts decoratively on top. Use any *left over piecrust* to make additional cutouts, sprinkle them with a mixture of sugar and cinnamon, and bake as above. These make great "cookies" to delight children and adults alike!

Filo dough bows make very pretty garnishes for foods encased in filo crusts. Marlene Sorosky, in *Cooking for Holidays and Celebrations*, tops filo-encased chicken breasts with these fragile, flaky bows. Her instructions are:

> "Place one sheet of filo on a damp towel, narrow side near you. Brush with butter. Cut into 3-inch strips. With fingers, crimp the center of each strip together down the length of the dough to form a bow. Place on baking sheet ... and bake at 400° for 5 to 8 minutes, or until golden brown. Watch carefully."

Store in an airtight container or freeze for future use.

Short Cuts for Easy, Last Minute Entertaining

When time is short and unexpected company arrives; when you feel unprepared, uncertain, uneasy, undecided; when you are unwilling to undertake the challenge of planning and creating an elaborate meal, *make it simple!*

Enjoy a truly casual affair – serve it from a buffet set up in the kitchen, or if you prefer, from the dining room, patio, porch or balcony.

Set up card tables if you need more room, or use TV tables or lap trays for those who do not like to balance plates on their laps. Roll the utensils in napkins or put them in baskets, bowls, or utensil holders, and place them near the plates.

If you need a quick centerpiece, use what you have on hand – a potted plant from your garden, a basket or bowl of fruit (or even vegetables) from the refrigerator. Embellish these with leaves from your prettiest trees or shrubs, or with parsley, cilantro, or carrot tops from the vegetable crisper. Place the parsley or cilantro in the centerpiece at the very last minute because they will wilt if left too long.

In many parts of the country you can *barbecue* most months during the year; if you have a porch or balcony overhang, you can even sizzle steaks in the rain. You can barbecue almost anything, from *beef* and *poultry* to *seafood* and *vegetable kabobs*, brushing them with your favorite homemade or bottled marinade. If you have time, marinate the beef or poultry first, for added flavor.

Serve the barbecued dinner with a simple *salad* and/or a fresh or frozen *vegetable*. For *dessert*, you might set out an assortment of left over cakes, cookies, pies, etc., plucked from your freezer. Ice creams and sherbets are delicious topped with fruit or liqueurs. Or you might prefer to purchase a sinfully rich concoction from your favorite bakery on your way home from work.

Sometimes, the easiest is the best – a barbecued steak, a baked potato, and a tossed green salad.

A good friend of mine barbecues *chicken* with a wonderful bottled sweet-and-sour sauce, serves it with a delicious and moist *corn bread* (which can be made from a mix), a tossed green salad, and for dessert, *ice cream bars*. Everyone loves it!

Keep bottled barbecue sauces on hand, and if you run out, mix equal parts of catsup, A-1 Sauce and water. If it sounds good to you, add a teaspoon of orange marmalade or grape jelly.

Not only is *horseradish* good for you, it also is delicious when added to shrimp cocktail sauce, mashed potatoes, deviled eggs, stews, soups and sauces, whether you grate it fresh or use it right out of the jar. ***Do not serve dishes containing horseradish in or on silver serving pieces.***

Lamb chops are a favorite of mine. Lather them with Dijon mustard, sprinkle them with herbs (such as Mayacamas herb mix, see page 34), and then barbecue them or bake them in a preheated 350° oven for about an hour, or until they are crispy and brown (they will, however, be well done). If taken straight out of the freezer, add 20 minutes to the baking time.

Chicken also can be basted with barbecue sauce and baked in the oven. Wild rice nicely complements any meat or fowl dish.

If you have *Boboli* (a pizza like crust found in most supermarkets) on hand, set up a pizza bar and offer different toppings, using whatever you have on hand in your pantry or refrigerator. If you don't have any tomato or spaghetti sauce, mix a little salsa and mayonnaise together; it will make a good base for your toppings. I always keep an extra Boboli or two in my freezer for last minute pizzas or appetizers.

Top *hot dogs* with homemade or canned chili, sauerkraut or beans. Add grated cheese and chopped onions. Serve *hamburgers* on half a bun and top them with combinations of herbed butter, crumbled bleu or grated cheddar cheese, chopped onions and guacamole, or baste them with homemade or bottled teriyaki marinade.

Set up an *ice cream bar* and serve various toppings from pitchers, plastic squeeze bottles, or pretty bowls, and let your guests decorate their own sundaes as they wish. Have side dishes of chopped nuts, chocolate bits, coconut, whipped cream, and whole stemmed maraschino cherries.

Or take a prebaked pie crust from the freezer and fill it with one or two layers of softened ice cream to make an ice cream pie. Top with any of a variety of sauces and refreeze it until you are ready for dessert.

If you have any leftover angel food cake in your freezer, butter wedges and put them under the broiler until they are golden brown. Top with liqueur flavored fruit if you wish.

Providing you have the available space, I would suggest that you keep at least the following on hand:

In your PANTRY (after opening, refrigerate to keep fresh):

- crackers and cookies
- pretzels, popcorn, potato chips and tortilla chips
- salt and pepper
- assortment of spices and herbs
- Parmesan cheese
- mayonnaise and mustards
- catsup
- tomato sauce, tomato paste and pasta sauce
- salsa (for toppings and dips)
- bottled barbecue sauce
- bottled salad dressings (creamy, or oil and vinegar)
- pastas
- tuna (for sandwiches, salads, tonato sauce and dips)
- coffee and tea
- soft drinks and mineral water
- chocolate sauce
- liqueurs
- Knorr's Crème Caramel (found in most markets)
- sugar (granulated, powdered and brown)
- flour (white, cake, unbleached and whole wheat)
- baking powder
- baking soda
- cocoa powder
- vanilla
- chocolate (unsweetened and semisweet)
- cherries (green and red)
- shredded coconut
- chocolate and butterscotch chips (for cookies, cakes, toppings)
- canned chicken, beef and vegetable broth
- rice (brown, white and wild)
- garlic cloves
- assorted nuts
- raisins, golden raisins and currants
- mixes (muffins, cakes, dips and salad dressings)

In your FREEZER:

- Boboli (or other brands of pizza crust)
- dips
- cheeses
- cookies, muffins, cakes and breads
- ice cream
- packaged fruits
- piecrusts or leftover piecrust dough
- lamb chops
- chicken breasts
- frozen vegetables (including freshly shredded carrots)
- leftover rices (reheat in a double boiler, steam or wrap in foil and heat in the oven)

As an aside, you may have heard that sugar or honey can be applied as an antiseptic to small, superficial wounds and as a drawing out "salve" for small splinters. Keep a small supply handy for such medicinal uses.

Cocktail Party Suggestions

If you are having a small cocktail/dinner party, let your guests mix their own drinks. They find it very relaxing and enjoy the opportunity to visit with old friends, or meet new ones, while mixing their drinks.

For large cocktail parties, it is best to hire a bartender(s) who will either mix and pass drinks or set up and tend the bar or bars. These should be conveniently located, yet out of the way of your mingling guests.

If you do not know of a good bartender, ask your friends. Your local liquor store is the next best source and probably has a list on hand. Be sure to inquire about the fee and find out what bar equipment will be supplied. Bartenders, as do caterers, generally expect a gratuity in addition to their fee.

Bar equipment should include a corkscrew, bottle opener, cocktail knife (for orange slices, lemon twists and lime wedges), cocktail shaker, ice bucket and tongs, wine cooler, jigger, long handled stirrer, and a pitcher for water. You should provide cocktail napkins, at least three per guest.

If you don't have your own, rent your glassware from your liquor store or a party store. You will need highball and old-fashioned glasses, and stemware for wine. Ice can be purchased from the liquor store, local market, or ice house.

You may wish to purchase the alcoholic and nonalcoholic beverages from a discount store. If you purchase them from your liquor store, they will help you determine the quantity you need, deliver it, and take back whatever you don't use; and if you run low during the party, a simple phone call will probably bring the needed replenishments in short order.

Have plenty of mixes (tonic water, soda water, 7-Up, orange juice, etc.) and plenty of soft drinks. Many people these days prefer mineral water, juices, sodas, diet beers, and wine. Also, it would be considerate to have some nonalcoholic beer and wine on hand for those who prefer it.

I have found that punch is not too popular at parties anymore, except at Christmas when eggnogs and wassail bowls are still a part of the tradition.

In addition to the more usual drinks during the holidays, you might wish to provide spiced cider served with cinnamon stick stirrers; or hot cocoa with peppermint candy cane stirrers. Float tiny marshmallows on top of the hot cocoa.

You might want to provide hot coffee as well (see More Special Touches, page 110).

Decide whether you want your cocktail party to be a casual open house or a formal celebration of an event or holiday. Send out your

invitations a month in advance unless you plan to invite your guests by telephone – then plan how extensive you want your menu to be.
In the pages that follow, I have provided some suggested menus and related recipes. Pick what appeals to you and add your own favorites.

A few words of caution

- Never serve caviar, vinegar, eggs, lemon or horseradish based dips, sauces or dressings, in or on silver – they chemically react with the metal and can possibly make your guests ill.

- To serve deviled eggs on a silver platter, wet the platter and cover it with a plastic wrap. Place a bed of lettuce or chopped greens on the plastic and rest the eggs on the lettuce/greens.

- Cocktail party fare is mostly finger food, so have plenty of cocktail napkins, as well as small plates, for your guests.

- When using silver pieces with your floral arrangements, line the silver container with heavy plastic to protect it from the planting soil and plant material which can damage the silver.

MENUS AND RECIPES

In this chapter I have outlined some menu suggestions for buffet or cocktail parties, luncheons and dinner parties with international and Hawaiian themes.

Following each of these menus, I have gathered together many of my favorite recipes which reflect the party themes. I'm sure you will find each of these recipes as delightful and delicious as I do.

Although presented in categories by party type and theme, I think you will find that all of the recipes included in this chapter have a much broader application than just the party category under which they have been listed.

As I have encouraged you in earlier chapters, be bold – experiment with different dishes, and serve them for nontraditional occasions and in varied settings.

I heartily endorse all the cookbooks, magazines and authors mentioned in this chapter or elsewhere in the book.

Finally, I should note that all of the recipes presented have been selected from my own personal recipe files, which I have been accumulating for many, many years. Where known, I have indicated my original source at the end of each recipe, and I wish to thank all those wonderful cooks.

MENU SUGGESTIONS FOR BUFFET
AND COCKTAIL PARTIES

Soups:
- cold gazpacho
- hot tomato
- hot tomato consommé with fresh dill

Sliced cold meats/ poultry:
- ham
- turkey
- roast beef

Cheeses:
- Swiss, sliced thin or cubed
- cheddar, sliced thin or cubed
- Brie, Camembert rounds or wedges
- cheese crock, served with apple slices
- herbed or plain cheese spreads

Menu Suggestions for Buffet and Cocktail Parties (continued)

Bread/rolls:
- tiny croissants
- baguettes of French bread
- soft rolls, split and buttered
- miniature corn muffins
- dark pumpernickel or rye bread

Spreads:
- butter in small containers
- mayonnaise in small containers
- horseradish in small containers
- mustards, several kinds, in small pots

Crackers:
- assortment of various crackers

Seafood:
- shrimp with cocktail sauce
- salmon, poached or smoked, served with water crackers, dilled mayonnaise, sour cream, lemon, chopped onion
- black caviar with triangles of toast, chopped white onions, and in separate dishes, chopped hard-boiled egg whites and yolks

Finger foods:

- pickled hard-boiled eggs
- tiny baked French lamb chops
- roasted marinated chicken wings
- cocktail meatballs
- deviled eggs with sliced pimiento-stuffed olives or caviar garnish
- miniature hot dogs or hamburgers

Nuts:
- salted pecans, almonds or mixed nuts

Menu Suggestions for Buffet and Cocktail Parties (continued)

Cold dips:
- guacamole with taco chips
- Mexican layered dip with taco chips
- melon platter with chutney dip
- spinach dip with crudities (raw vegetables)

Hot dips:
- cheese-onion dip with crackers
- artichoke dip with corn chips
- bean dip Mexicana

Cold vegetables:
- zesty marinated carrots
- carrots with dill

Fresh vegetable platter:
- pea pods
- sliced celery, carrots, zucchini
- jicama sticks
- broccoli florets
- asparagus spears
- Belgian endive

Hot appetizers:
- Gougère (puffed cheese pastry)
- cheese-stuffed potato skins
- filo triangles
- cheese puffs with chipped beef
- empanadas
- cheese rounds
- taco tartlets

Desserts:
- small lemon curd tarts (see page 172)
- chocolate-dipped strawberries

RECOMMENDED RECIPES FOR BUFFET AND COCKTAIL PARTIES

Hot Cheese-Onion Dip

Ingredients:

> 1 1/2 cups sharp cheddar cheese, grated
> 1 1/2 cups mayonnaise
> 1 1/2 cups onion, chopped

Mix ingredients in shallow 1 1/2 quart casserole or baking dish. Bake in 350° oven for about 20 minutes or until the mixture bubbles. Serve with crackers. (Barbara Sargeant)

Hot Artichoke Dip

Ingredients:

> 1 6 ounce jar marinated artichokes, coarsely chopped
> 1 7 ounce can regular artichokes, coarsely chopped
> 1 4 ounce can green chilies, diced
> 1 cup Parmesan cheese, grated
> 1 cup mayonnaise
> cheddar or Monterey jack cheese, grated

Except for the cheddar or Monterey jack cheese, mix all ingredients in a 1 1/2 quart casserole or baking dish. Cover with grated cheddar or Monterey jack. Cook for 5 minutes in a microwave oven set at high level. Serve with corn chips. (Susan Bansmer)

Bean Dip Mexicana

Ingredients:

> 2 1 pound cans kidney beans
> 1/4 cup salad oil
> 1 cup cheddar cheese, grated
> 1/2 teaspoon salt
> 1 1/2 teaspoons chili powder

Drain kidney beans, saving the liquid. Heat oil in a skillet. Add beans and mash with a fork. Add 1/3 cup of the bean liquid to help make a smoother mixture. Stir in the cheese, salt and chili powder. Cook over medium heat, stirring all the while, until cheese has melted. If mixture gets too stiff for dipping, stir in a little more bean liquid. Serve hot with corn chips. Makes about 2 cups of dip.   (Lucille Maxwell)

Mexican Layered Dip

Ingredients:

> 1 16 ounce can refried beans mixed with
> 1/2 teaspoon chili powder
> 1 large avocado, skinned, mashed and mixed with a
>   few drops of lemon juice
> 3 green onions, chopped
> 1/2 cup ripe olives, chopped
> 1 7 ounce can or bottle green chili salsa
> 1 8 ounce carton sour cream mixed with
>   1 package taco seasoning to taste
> grated cheddar cheese

In a shallow, 2 quart, glass or ceramic serving dish or bowl, layer the ingredients in the order listed, with the grated cheddar cheese added last so it covers the entire dip. Refrigerate until ready to serve. Serve cold with tortilla chips.

Guacamole

Plan on one half avocado for each person. Mash avocados until slightly chunky. Add 1/2 teaspoon lemon juice for each avocado, and stir in salsa, either mild or hot, to taste. To make the guacamole creamier, add a dollop of sour cream. Serve with taco chips.

Kaleidoscope of Brie

Remove the top rind of a small round of Brie cheese and lightly mark 4 quadrants (triangles) with a knife. Sprinkle cracked pepper over the first quarter, paprika or cayenne over the second, chopped parsley or green onions over the third, and chopped spiced cranberry relish and toasted chopped almonds over the fourth. Serve at room temperature with crackers.

Cocktail Sauce for Shrimp

To 1 cup of homemade or bottled chili sauce, mix 1 1/2 heaping teaspoons of prepared horseradish and 1 1/2 teaspoons of lemon juice. Serves 6 to 8 people, assuming 3 to 4 shrimp per person.

Cocktail Dip for Shrimp and Raw Vegetables

Mix to taste mayonnaise and curry powder or dill (fresh or dried). Place dip in individual bowls in the center of a platter and surround with shrimp and/or raw vegetables. 1 cup of dip will serve about 6 to 8 people.

Spinach Dip with Crudities

Ingredients:

> 1 package frozen chopped spinach
> **or**
> 2 cups fresh spinach, finely chopped
> 1 cup sour cream
> 1/2 cup mayonnaise
> 1/2 cup fresh parsley, minced
> 1/2 cup green onions (white part only), minced
> 1/2 teaspoon Beau Monde seasoning
> 1/2 teaspoon dried dill weed
> salt and pepper to taste
> 1 small head red cabbage
> endive, cucumber, zucchini, carrots, celery,
>   cauliflower and snow peas

Cook the frozen spinach according to the package instructions, or if using fresh spinach, cook in a 2 quart saucepan for 6 to 10 minutes and drain thoroughly. In a bowl, mix together sour cream, mayonnaise, parsley, green onions and spices. Add spinach and stir thoroughly, then taste for seasoning. Refrigerate overnight or longer (dip must be prepared at least 24 hours before serving to allow the ingredients to blend). Place the spinach dip in the hollowed out center of the cabbage head, and serve with chilled Belgian endive leaves; cucumber, zucchini and carrot spears; sliced celery stalks; snow peas; radishes and cauliflower. Serves 6 to 8.

(*California Heritage Cookbook*, Pasadena Junior League)

Author's note: Leftover spinach dip is delicious as a topping for baked or broiled tomato halves.

Melon Platter with Chutney Dip

Ingredients:

> 2   8 ounce packages cream cheese
> 1/4 cup dry sherry wine
> 1   teaspoon salt
> 1/2 teaspoon curry powder
> 1/3 cup chopped chutney
> 1/2 to 1 cup sour cream
> honeydew or cantaloupe balls

Soften cheese. Blend in sherry, salt, curry and chutney. Stir in sour cream and chill. Place dip in bowl and surround with melon balls. Serve with tooth picks.

Salted Pecans

Place 1 pound shelled pecans in a mixing bowl and add 1/4 cup cooking oil. Stir to coat the pecans well. Remove the pecans with a slotted spoon and spread evenly on a sided cookie sheet. Place in a preheated 300° oven for 10 minutes. Remove from oven, stir pecans while on the cookie sheet, again spreading them evenly. Return to the oven for 10 more minutes. Remove from oven, salt liberally and stir. Drain on paper towels.

Salted Almonds

Place 1 pound almonds, shelled and skinned, in a mixing bowl and add 2 tablespoons cooking oil. Stir to coat the almonds well. Remove the almonds with a slotted spoon and spread evenly on a sided cookie sheet. Place in a preheated 325° oven for 10 minutes. Remove from oven and turn oven off. Stir almonds while on the cookie sheet, again spreading them evenly. Return to the oven for 15 more minutes. Remove from oven, salt liberally and stir. Drain on paper towels.

Artichokes Filled with Red Caviar

Using cooked or canned artichoke bottoms, arrange on a bed of lettuce (at Christmas add a touch of greens or holly) and fill each bottom with 1 tablespoon sour cream. Sprinkle with chopped green onions, and top with 1 teaspoon red caviar. Serve chilled.

Carrots with Dill

Skin and slice raw carrots into sticks. Crisp in water in the refrigerator. Drain. Sprinkle with dried dill. Serve chilled.

Zesty Marinated Carrots

Ingredients:

> raw carrots, about 1 pound
> boiling water
> 2 bay leaves
> 1 package Good Season Zesty Italian dressing mix
> 1/4 cup white wine vinegar
> 3/4 cup water
> 1/2 teaspoon each mustard seed and dried dill weed
> 1 clove garlic, minced

Skin and slice carrots into sticks. Cover and steam carrots for 6 to 8 minutes until al dente, or tender-crisp. Drain. Blend the package of Zesty Italian dressing mix, vinegar, water, mustard seed, dill weed and garlic in a one quart jar, and shake vigorously. Place carrots in with the marinade. Tuck in bay leaves, cover, and refrigerate for 6 to 8 hours, shaking once in a while. Serve chilled.

These marinated carrots can be kept refrigerated for up to two weeks.

Vegetable Platter

Either with or without dips, arrange groupings of fresh vegetables consisting of: sliced celery, carrots, and zucchini; cauliflower sections and jicama sticks; fresh pea pods; broccoli florets; asparagus spears; leaves of Belgian endive. Garnish with parsley or edible flowers.

Gougère (puffed cheese pastry)

Ingredients:

1 cup water
1/4 pound (1 stick) butter, cut into pieces
1 cup all purpose flour
4 eggs
1 1/2 cups Gruyère cheese, grated
1 teaspoon Dijon mustard
1/2 teaspoon dry mustard
1/3 cup green onions, sliced (optional)
1/3 cup slivered or sliced almonds

Combine water and butter in a medium saucepan and bring to a rolling boil over high heat. Add flour all at once and beat with a wooden spoon until mixture forms a ball and leaves the sides of the pan. Remove from heat. Add eggs one at a time, beating well after each addition, until dough is shiny and smooth. Blend in one cup of the cheese, the mustards and onions (optional). On a lightly greased baking sheet, form an 8 inch circle by dropping tablespoons of dough with the sides touching each other. Repeat, making a second layer by placing tablespoons of dough on top of the first layer. Sprinkle the ring of dough with the remaining cheese and the almonds. Bake in a preheated 400º oven for 30 minutes or until puffed up, golden brown and hollow sounding when tapped on the side. Cut into wedges. Serves 8 to 10.

Cheese-Stuffed Potato Skins

Scrub and pierce small red potatoes with a fork, allowing 2 potatoes per person. Place on a baking sheet and bake in a preheated 400° oven for about one hour, or until tender. Cool. Cut in half crosswise and remove the pulp, leaving a 1/8 inch thick shell. Save the pulp for some other future use. Brush the potato skins lightly with melted butter. Fill with a mixture of shredded Monterey jack and cheddar cheeses. Sprinkle with chopped green onions (optional). Refrigerate until ready to bake. Bake in a preheated 400° oven until the cheese has melted. Serve with dishes of sour cream, salsa and chopped green onions.

Antipasto Tray

A selection of broccoli, asparagus (with or without dips), large pimiento-stuffed green olives, caper berries, deviled eggs, marinated miniature corn, salami, cheeses, tangy pickles, red onion rings, Mexican peppers, marinated artichoke hearts, marinated carrots or crunchy raw carrots sprinkled with dill, cherry tomatoes plain or, if you wish, stuffed with dilled cream cheese, spicy egg salad or crabmeat salad.

Pickled hard-boiled Eggs

Pour the contents of a can or jar of pickled beets into a bowl and add shelled hard-boiled eggs and sliced white or red onions. Cover and refrigerate from 1 to 3 days. Remove from refrigerator and drain off juice. Cut eggs in half lengthwise. Serve on a bed of lettuce.

For decorative (red colored) and tasty deviled eggs, prepare pickled eggs as above and drain, then proceed as you would in making your favorite deviled egg recipe.

Filo Triangles

Filo is fun, and not as hard to work with as you might think. The most important thing to remember is not to let it dry out. While using filo, keep it under a moist, but not wet, dish towel; if it falls apart while you are forming it, just piece it together or patch it with more filo and continue on – the finished product will look and taste as though you had never made a repair.

A book titled *The Art of Filo Cookbook* by Marti Sousanis is a must if you really want to get involved with this flaky and very tasty pastry.

Keep filo dough in the freezer until you are ready to use it. Transfer it to the refrigerator the day before you need it. After the filo has thawed, remove the amount you will need and refreeze the rest.

Cut the sheets into lengthwise strips about 2 to 3 inches wide. Brush with melted butter or oil and place about a teaspoonful of filling in the center at one end of the strip. Fold one corner over the filling making a triangle, then fold the other corner, as in folding a flag. Repeat until you have used up the entire strip. Brush the top lightly with melted butter or oil. Bake in preheated 375° oven for 20 minutes.

These filo triangles can be made ahead and frozen until needed. Move to the refrigerator the night before your party and bake them just before serving.

There are many fillings for filo triangles such as cheddar cheese, feta cheese, boursin cheese, and spicy cream cheese either plain or mixed with chopped shrimp. Marinated artichokes make an easy and very popular filling. Drain the artichokes, using the marinade instead of melted butter to brush the filo. Place a small piece of artichoke in the center of the strip of filo at one end and fold into a triangle as described above.

Cheese Puffs Filled with Chipped Beef

Ingredients for cheese puffs:

>2 tablespoons butter or margarine
>1/4 cup boiling water
>1/4 cup all purpose flour, sifted
>Dash of salt
>1 egg
>1/4 cup Swiss cheese, shredded

In a small saucepan, melt butter. Add water, flour and salt. Stir vigorously until mixture pulls away from the sides of the pan and forms a ball. Cool slightly. Add egg and beat until mixture is smooth. Stir in cheese. Drop level teaspoons of dough on a greased cookie sheet. Bake in preheated 400° oven 20 minutes. Remove from oven, split and cool. Fill puffs with chipped beef filling.

Ingredients for chipped beef filling:

>1   3 1/2 ounce package (about 1 cup) chipped beef,
>   shredded
>1/2 cup celery, finely chopped
>2 tablespoons green pepper, finely chopped
>1/2 teaspoon prepared horseradish
>1/3 cup mayonnaise

Mix ingredients together thoroughly and fill each puff with the chipped beef filling.

Cheese Rounds

Ingredients:

> 2 3 ounce packages cream cheese
> 2 egg yolks
> 1 teaspoon onion juice
> 1/2 teaspoon Worcestershire sauce

Mix ingredients and set aside. Using a round biscuit or cookie cutter, cut small rounds from slices of white bread (3 or 4 rounds from one slice of bread). Freeze the bread first; it will make it easier to cut. Toast the rounds of bread on both sides under the broiler. Place cheese mixture on top of the rounds and broil until puffy and golden brown.

Cocktail Meatballs

Ingredients:

> 1 pound ground beef
> 1 egg, slightly beaten
> 1/4 cup fine, dry bread crumbs
> 1/2 onion, finely chopped
> 1 teaspoon salt
> 1/4 teaspoon pepper
> 2 tablespoons oil
> 1 12 ounce bottle chili sauce
> 1 10 ounce jar grape jelly
> 1 teaspoon lemon juice
> 1 teaspoon brown sugar

Combine beef, egg, bread crumbs, onion, salt and pepper. Form into balls the size of a walnut. Heat oil in a skillet and brown meatballs on all sides. In a saucepan, stir together chili sauce, jelly, lemon juice and brown sugar. Bring mixture to a boil, stirring constantly. Add meatballs, cover and simmer for 30 minutes. Serve warm from a chafing dish.   (Lucille Maxwell)

Cheese Crock

Ingredients:

> 1 pound cheddar cheese, finely shredded
> 1/2 cup sherry wine or brandy
> 1/4 cup whipping cream
> 1 tablespoon parsley, chopped
> 2 tablespoons green onions, chopped
> 1/2 to 3/4 cup pecans, walnuts or pistachios, chopped
> dash of cayenne pepper

Mix ingredients thoroughly. Place in crock or serving container. Refrigerate (to age) for several days. Bring to room temperature before serving. Serve with crackers and apple slices. Makes about 2 1/2 cups.

Taco Tartlets

Tartlet shells:

Using a fork, mix together 1/2 pint sour cream, 2 tablespoons taco sauce, 2 ounces chopped ripe olives and 3/4 cup coarsely crunched tortilla chips. Press into 1/2 inch mini muffin cups.

Tartlet filling:

Mix together 1 pound ground beef, 2 tablespoons taco seasoning mix and 1 tablespoon water. Place a spoonful of mixture in each shell, mounding slightly. Sprinkle 1 cup shredded cheddar cheese over the tops. Bake in preheated 425° oven for 7 to 8 minutes. Gently remove from muffin cups with the tip of a knife. Serve hot. Makes about 30 tartlets.

Empanadas (turnovers)

Ingredients for empanadas pastry (if not purchased premade):

> 3 cups flour
> 1 1/2 teaspoons salt
> 1/2 cup shortening
> 6 to 7 tablespoons water

Stir together flour and salt. Cut in shortening until fine and the size of small peas. Sprinkle with water, one tablespoon at a time, mixing with a fork until a dough forms.

Ingredients for empanadas filling:

> olive oil
> 1 large onion, chopped medium fine (1 cup)
> 1 medium green pepper, seeded and chopped fine (3/4
>   cup)
> 1 clove garlic, minced
> 1 pound ground beef
> 1 small potato, cooked, pared and diced (3/4 cup)
> 1/2 cup raisins
> 3/4 teaspoon dried thyme
> salt and pepper to taste
> 2 hard-boiled eggs, finely chopped

In a medium skillet with a little oil, cook onion, green pepper and garlic until wilted. Add beef, mash with a fork and cook until red color disappears. Stir in potato, raisins, eggs, thyme, salt and pepper. Roll out pastry dough. Using a 3 inch biscuit cutter, cut out rounds. Spoon beef mixture into the center of each round. Fold pastry over filling so that edges meet. Crimp with a fork to seal, dipping the fork in water occasionally to help make the seal. Bake in a preheated 450° oven for about 15 minutes or until golden brown.

(Los Angeles Times, Food Section)

Chocolate-Dipped Strawberries

Melt 3 ounces of semisweet chocolate with 1/2 cup half-and-half in the top of a double boiler over hot, but not boiling water. Remove from heat and add 2 tablespoons of orange-flavored liqueur. Dip large strawberries, with stems left on, into the mixture and tap lightly on the side of the pan to remove excess. Place on a wax paper-lined baking sheet and refrigerate. Makes 1 to 2 dozen strawberries, depending on the size.

Hot Mulled Punch (Nonalcoholic)

Ingredients:

    5 cans (about 12 ounces each) apple juice
    3 2 inch sticks cinnamon
    1 tablespoon nutmeg
    6 pints cranberry juice cocktail
    1 pint orange juice
    1 pint grapefruit juice
    2 oranges
    1 lemon
    whole cloves
    1 1/2 cups honey

Pour apple juice into a kettle. Add cinnamon and nutmeg and simmer for 20 minutes. Add cranberry juice cocktail, orange and grapefruit juices. Stud oranges and lemon with cloves and drop into mixture. Heat until boiling and stir in honey. Heat punch bowl, ***particularly if it is glass or crystal,*** by filling with warm water and letting it stand for a few minutes. Empty bowl of water and fill with heated punch and fruit. Makes about 2 gallons of punch.

Nonalcoholic Cucumber and Tomato Juice Cocktail

Slice one large cucumber and remove seeds. Grate and measure. For each one part of grated cucumber, add 3 parts tomato juice. Add the juice of 1 lemon. Stir. Serve chilled.

Wassail Bowl (alcoholic)

Ingredients:

> 4 baking apples, cored
> 16 lumps sugar
> 1 teaspoon coriander
> 2 lemons, sliced thin
> 12 cups sherry wine
> 24 whole cloves
> 1 teaspoon ginger
> 1 teaspoon nutmeg
> 1/2 cup sugar
> 1 cup water
> 6 eggs at room temperature, separated

Peel apples down one inch from the top and stick cloves into the peeled portion. Insert 4 lumps of sugar into each apple cavity. Bake, basting frequently with the juice from the apples, in a preheated 325° oven about 40 minutes or until tender. In a large kettle combine spices, sugar, lemon slices and water. Bring to a boil and simmer for 3 minutes. Add sherry and allow to continue simmering. Meanwhile, beat egg whites until stiff. Beat egg yolks until thick, then fold in egg whites. Mix a small amount of the hot liquid with the egg mixture so that it does not curdle or become lumpy. Combine the rest of the hot liquid with the egg mixture in the kettle. Serve hot in a preheated punch bowl with roasted apples floating on the surface. Serves about 16.

Eggnog (nonalcoholic)

Ingredients:

> 3 eggs, at room temperature
> 3/4 cup sugar
> 1/4 teaspoon salt
> 4 cups milk, scalded
> 1/2 teaspoon vanilla
> pinch of salt
> nutmeg, freshly grated

Separate eggs. Place yolks in large mixing bowl; place the whites in two separate bowls, half in each, and set aside. Stir egg yolks lightly then stir in sugar and 1/4 teaspoon salt. Slowly stir in milk. Heat in a double boiler, stirring constantly, until the mixture coats the back of a spoon (about 15 minutes).

Remove from heat and stir in vanilla. Beat half of the egg whites until stiff and fold into mixture. Beat until smooth. Pour mixture into serving bowl and chill.

Just prior to serving, add a pinch of salt to the remaining half of the egg whites and beat until stiff. Spoon "icebergs" of egg white on top of the mixture and dust liberally with freshly grated nutmeg. Serve in eggnog cups with demitasse spoons for eating the icebergs.
Serves 6 to 8.   (Nancy Nashu)

Eggnog (alcoholic)

Ingredients:

> 6 eggs
> 1 quart half-and-half
> 2 cups milk
> 2 cups bourbon
> 1 cup Myers dark Jamaican rum
> 1/2 to 1 cup powdered sugar
> pinch salt
> nutmeg, freshly grated

Separate eggs. Place yolks in large mixing bowl; place whites in separate bowl and set aside. Beat egg yolks lightly until smooth. Stir in half-and-half and milk. Beat until uniformly creamy in color. Add bourbon and rum, stirring well. Add 1/2 cup powdered sugar and stir well. Taste. Add more sugar to taste, up to a total of 1cup, stirring well with each addition. Pour into serving bowl.

Add a pinch of salt to the egg whites and beat until stiff. Spoon "icebergs" of egg white onto the mixture. Dust liberally with freshly grated nutmeg. Serve in eggnog cups with demitasse spoons. Serves 12 to 14.

LUNCHEON MENU SUGGESTIONS

Drinks:
- dry white wine
- sparkling mineral water with lemon or lime slices
- Bloody Marys

Nibbles:
- salted almonds (see page 129)
- cheese cookies

Entrées:
- a combination of each of the following served on beds of lettuce:
    - ☐ chicken salad served on pineapple or melon ring, and
    - ☐ shrimp remoulade garnished with Belgian endive, and
    - ☐ deviled eggs garnished with edible flowers
- avocado pie, deviled eggs garnished with caviar, sliced pimientos or carrot "flowers," all served on a bed of leafy lettuce. Add a thick slice of tomato with a dollop of herbed mayonnaise, garnish with a caper berry or watercress
- chicken salad served in a pineapple "bowl" with a small scoop of any flavor sherbet on top or alongside in a small ramekin

Luncheon Menu Suggestions (continued)

Breads:
- muffins or rolls, split and buttered

Beverages:
- iced tea with lemon slices
- coffee, regular or decaffeinated
- white wine
- sparkling mineral water

Desserts:
- French chocolate cake cut in wedges and served with *crème anglaise* or whipped cream and candy garnish
- chocolate mousse garnished with whipped cream and chocolate curls served with dainty cookies
- sherbet balls in several flavors and colors, either in cookie cups or separately, with brown sugar cookies

RECOMMENDED RECIPES FOR LUNCHEONS

Cheese Cookies

Ingredients:

> 1 5 ounce jar Kraft's Sharp Cheese, softened
> 1/4 pound (1 stick) butter, softened
> 1 cup plus 2 tablespoons flour
> 1/2 cup pecans, chopped
> paprika

Blend cheese with butter. Add flour and pecans and stir until thoroughly blended. Refrigerate until chilled, or at least one hour. Roll into walnut-size balls. With the palm of your hand, flatten to 1/4 inch thick round. Sprinkle with paprika. Bake in a preheated 350° oven for 18 minutes. Can be made ahead, baked and frozen for future use. If frozen, unthaw and warm in a preheated 350° oven for about 10 minutes before serving. Makes about 3 dozen.

Cold Avocado Seafood Quiche

Ingredients for quiche:

> 1 medium ripe avocado, coarsely chopped
> 1 7 ounce can artichoke hearts, chopped
> 1/4 pound fresh crabmeat, cooked and shredded
> 1/4 pound ham, cooked and coarsely chopped
> 1 tablespoon capers, rinsed and drained
> 2 teaspoons tomato sauce
> 1 teaspoon lemon juice
> 4 to 6 medium shrimps, deveined, cooked and chopped
> 1 1/2 cups dressing (see below)
> 1 *pâté brisee* baked pie shell (see below)

Mix the first nine ingredients in a large bowl. Spoon into pie shell. To decorate and designate individual servings, place thin slices of

avocado and halves of shrimp, sliced lengthwise, around the quiche as spokes of a wheel. A small sprig of dill can be added to the avocado and shrimp.

Ingredients for quiche dressing:

> 1/2 cup mayonnaise
> 1 teaspoon white vinegar
> 1 teaspoon Dijon mustard
> 1 garlic clove, minced
> salt and pepper to taste

Combine ingredients and mix thoroughly.

Ingredients for quiche pâté brisee (pie shell):

> 1 1/2 cups all purpose flour
> pinch of salt
> 5 1/2 tablespoons unsalted butter
> 3 tablespoons vegetable shortening
> 1/4 cup ice water

Have all ingredients chilled. Sift flour and salt. If using a food processor, combine butter and shortening. Add water a little at a time to form a soft, pliable – though not sticky – dough. If mixing by hand in a mixing bowl, cut in butter and shortening with sifted flour and salt, using 2 knives, until mixture resembles coarse meal. Mix in water with a fork a little at a time and, with your hands, shape mixture into a ball. Flatten into a circle and enfold in plastic wrap. Chill for a few hours. On a lightly floured surface, roll pastry to 1/8 inch thickness. Place in an 8 inch by 10 inch quiche pan and trim off excess pastry. Prick bottom and sides with a fork. Line with aluminum foil. Weight with beans, rice or pie weights. Bake in a preheated 400° oven for 15 to 20 minutes. When the pastry begins to color around the edges, remove the weights and foil and continue to bake until the pastry is golden in color and dry. Cover the outer edges of the pastry with foil to keep them from getting too brown. Cool. The pie shell can be made ahead of time and frozen.

Chicken Salad

Barbara Tropp, *restaurateur*, prepares chicken breasts for cold chicken salads by immersing them in water flavored with peppercorns, onions and a little ginger. Submerge the chicken in a pot of flavored boiling water. Immediately turn off the heat, cover the pot, and leave until the water cools and the chicken is tender, about 2 hours. To make the salad, dice the chicken and add mayonnaise, chopped green onions, celery, toasted and slivered almonds, and a little curry (optional). Or try putting 2 quarts of chicken salad in a broiler-proof baking dish and cover with a mixture of 1 cup shredded cheddar cheese and 2 cups crushed potato chips. Place under the broiler for a few minutes until bubbling and brown. Allow at least 1/2 chicken breast for each person.

Shrimp Remoulade

Ingredients:

- 1 bunch green onions
- 2 stalks celery, strings removed
- 2 sprigs parsley
- 3 tablespoons Dijon mustard
- 4 teaspoons paprika
- 1 teaspoon salt
- 1 teaspoon fresh basil or 1/2 teaspoon dry basil
- 1/2 teaspoon pepper
- 1/4 teaspoon cayenne
- 6 tablespoons white vinegar
- 1 teaspoon lemon juice
- 3/4 cup olive oil
- 1 pound shrimp, deveined and cooked

In a food processor, chop onion, celery and parsley until almost a purée. Transfer to a bowl and add mustard, paprika, salt, pepper, basil, cayenne, vinegar, and lemon juice. Blend well. Slowly beat in olive oil and pour over shrimp. Refrigerate until ready to serve. The remoulade can be used as a dip for shrimp in lieu of a cocktail sauce.

Brown Sugar Cookies

Ingredients:

> 1/2 pound (2 sticks) unsalted butter at room
>   temperature, cut into 16 pieces
> 3/4 cup dark brown sugar
> yolk of 1 large egg
> 1 tablespoon pure vanilla extract
> 1 cup plus 2 tablespoons all purpose flour
> 1/4 teaspoon salt
> 1/2 cup granulated sugar

In a food processor, process butter and brown sugar with a metal blade about 20 seconds, until creamy, scraping down the work bowl as necessary. Add the egg yolk and vanilla. Pulse the food processor 5 times, then process for 10 seconds. Pulse in the flour and salt, scraping down the work bowl as necessary. Refrigerate for one hour. Shape into 1 inch balls and place about 2 inches apart on ungreased cookie sheet. Butter the bottom of a drinking glass, dip into sugar, and flatten cookies to about 1/4 inch thickness. Dip the glass into the sugar often while flattening the cookies. Bake in preheated 350° oven for about 12 minutes or until golden brown. Remove to a wire rack. Cool. Store in an airtight container. Makes 30.

(Judith Pacht, *The Pleasure of Cooking*)

Authors note: These cookies can also be made using a hand mixer rather than a food processor.

GREEK PARTY THEME

Flag Colors

- blue
- white

Party Occasions

- a trip to Greece
- a birthday party or honoring a friend
- any informal gathering

MENU SUGGESTIONS

Appetizer:
- filo triangles with feta cheese (see page 133)

Entrée:
- moussaka

Salad:
- mixed greens with feta cheese, toasted pine nuts, Greek olives (optional), tossed with a creamy or oil and vinegar dressing

Breads/rolls:
- French bread
- muffins: rosemary or lemon

Desserts:
- baklava, served with Ouzo (a potent Greek liqueur)
- lemon ice with sugar cookies (sprinkle cookies with a mixture of cinnamon, sugar and allspice before baking)

RECOMMENDED RECIPES

Moussaka

Ingredients:

>   2 pounds ground beef or lamb
>   3 tablespoons water
>   1 small onion, chopped
>   2 teaspoons salt
>   1/2 whole nutmeg, grated
>   1 6 ounce can tomato paste
>   1 green pepper, chopped
>   1/2 cup salad oil
>   8 small zucchinis, chopped
>   2 small eggplants , peeled and chopped
> **or**
>   2 large eggplants if you omit the zucchinis
>   1/2 pound Parmesan cheese, freshly grated

Place meat in a fry pan with water. Cook over medium heat for 10 minutes, stirring all the while. Add onions, salt, nutmeg and tomato paste. Bring to a boil then simmer for 20 minutes, stirring occasionally. Heat oil in a separate fry pan. Trim ends of zucchini, peel eggplant and slice both. Add to oil in fry pan, cover and cook until tender. (If using large eggplant, peel, slice and fry a few slices at a time in heated oil until they are tender).

Spread vegetable mixture in large flat casserole and sprinkle with 1/3 of the Parmesan cheese. Spread the meat mixture over the top. Sprinkle another 1/3 of the Parmesan over the top. Spoon the cream sauce (see below) over the meat and vegetable mixture. Combine the remaining Parmesan cheese with the bread crumbs and spread over the top. Bake in a preheated 350° oven for 1 hour. Serves 8 to 10.

Ingredients for moussaka cream sauce:

>   6 tablespoons butter
>   6 tablespoons flour
>   1/2 teaspoon salt
>   dash of nutmeg, grated
>   3 cups milk
>   3 eggs
>   Parmesan cheese saved from the moussaka recipe (see
>   above)
>   1/2 cup soft bread crumbs

Melt butter and remove from heat. Stir in flour, salt and nutmeg. Add milk gradually and bring back to a boil, stirring constantly, until thickened. Remove from heat. Beat eggs in a small bowl, then beat in a little of the hot cream sauce. Then add the egg mixture to the cream sauce, stir, and heat until thick – but do not boil! Spoon cream sauce over the moussaka meat and vegetable mixture (see above).

Baklava

Ingredients:

>   4 cups walnuts, finely chopped
>   3/4 cups sugar
>   2 teaspoons cinnamon
>   1 teaspoon allspice
>   1 pound filo pastry
>   1 pound unsalted butter, melted

Mix walnuts with sugar, cinnamon and allspice. Cut filo pastry sheets to fit a baking pan 10 inches by 15 inches, and 1 1/2 inches deep. Brush pan with melted butter. Place six sheets of filo in the bottom of the pan, one at a time, brushing each sheet with melted butter before adding the next sheet. Cover each sheet with a thin layer of the walnut mixture, cover that with a single sheet of filo, and brush with melted butter. Repeat this process, adding layers one at a time, until you have used up all the walnut mixture, but making sure that you have six

sheets of filo pastry left. Place these on top, one at a time, brushing each with melted butter before adding the next sheet.

With a sharp knife dipped in hot butter, cut the baklava diagonally into strips about 1 1/2 inches wide, then diagonally again in the other direction, about 1 1/2 inches wide, forming diamond-shaped pieces. Heat the remaining butter and pour into the knife slits between the diamond shaped pieces. Bake in a preheated 300° oven for 1 hour. When baklava is slightly browned, remove from oven and pour boiling syrup (see below) over it slowly, saving a little syrup for later. Increase the oven temperature to 400° and return the baklava to the oven for a few minutes or until the syrup has penetrated and the top is golden brown.

Remove from the oven and pour remaining syrup over the top. Keep in cool place until served. Makes about three dozen diamond-shaped pieces.

Ingredients for baklava syrup:

> 1 cup sugar
> 2 cups water
> 1 1/2 cups honey
> 2 teaspoons vanilla

Combine sugar and water and cook over low heat until syrupy, about 15 minutes. Add honey and vanilla, and cook for another 5 minutes. Pour over baklava (see above) while hot.

ITALIAN PARTY THEME

Flag Colors

- green
- white
- red

Party Occasions

- a trip to Italy
- a birthday party or honoring a friend
- a Christmas party (using the red and green flag colors)
- any informal gathering

MENU SUGGESTIONS

Appetizer:
- Boboli mini pizzas
- mixed nuts

Entrée:
- chicken lasagna
- make-your-own pizza bar

Salad:
- mixed greens with pitted and sliced black olives, sliced pimiento-stuffed green olives, halved cherry tomatoes, sliced green peppers, artichoke hearts, cubes of mozzarella cheese, slices of avocado and thin strips of salami, tossed with an oil and vinegar dressing
- antipasto tray

Breads/rolls:
- Italian hard crusted bread with butter
- garlic bread

Dessert:
- Neapolitan ice cream
- Make-your-own ice cream sundae bar

RECOMMENDED RECIPES

Chicken Lasagna

Ingredients:

> 1 package lasagna, uncooked
> 1/2 pound fresh mushrooms, washed and sliced
> 7 tablespoons butter
> 1 1/2 cups dry vermouth
> 4 tablespoons flour
> 4 cups whole milk
> 1 teaspoon fresh tarragon, chopped
> salt and pepper to taste
> 5 cups chicken, cooked, boned and shredded
> 2 cups mozzarella cheese, shredded

Cook lasagna as specified on the package until just tender, drain well and set aside. Sauté mushrooms in 3 tablespoons butter for about 3 minutes. Add 1 1/4 cups of vermouth and allow to simmer until the vermouth has almost completely evaporated. Set aside. Melt the remaining 4 tablespoons of butter in a saucepan. Stir in the flour and cook until bubbly. Gradually stir in the milk and cook over low heat, stirring constantly, until thick and creamy. Stir in the mushrooms, remaining 1/4 cup of vermouth and the tarragon. Add salt and pepper to taste. Simmer for about 3 minutes and set aside. Grease a 9 inch by 13 inch bake dish. Place a layer of cooked lasagna on the bottom of the dish, then a layer of chicken. Pour some of the vermouth sauce over the top, and sprinkle with cheese. Repeat these layers several times, ending with the cheese layer. Bake in a preheated 350° oven for about 40 to 45 minutes, or until bubbly and crusty on top. Makes about 8 servings.   (David Chaparro)

Make-Your-Own Pizza

Provide individual Boboli (or other favorite brand) pizza crust rounds and an assortment of pizza toppings, such as:

- tomato sauce (mix a little tomato paste into a premade sauce to thicken it)
- pepperoni, salami and prosciutto, sliced thin
- provolone, mozzarella, cheddar and Parmesan cheeses, grated
- onions, diced
- anchovies
- black olives, pitted and sliced or diced
- green pepper, sliced or diced
- mushrooms, sliced
- tomatoes, chopped
- fresh oregano, crumbled
- fresh basil, crushed
- olive oil lightly "scented" with garlic salt
- chicken, cooked and diced
- mayonnaise with a light addition of pesto sauce

Allow your guests to make their own pizzas by lathering the rounds with sauces selected, adding cheeses and toppings as desired, then baking them in preheated 450° oven for 8 to 10 minutes, until the crust is crisp and the cheese is melted.

Antipasto Tray

Ingredients:

- marinated mushrooms
- whole cherry tomatoes
- marinated carrots and zucchini
- marinated green and red peppers
- garbanzo beans
- marinated artichokes
- marinated baby ears of corn
- marinated eggplant
- black olives, preferably pitted
- pimiento-stuffed green olives
- salami and ham, thinly sliced and rolled into cornucopias
- mozzarella cheese, thinly sliced
- ricotta cheese, mounded in the center of the tray
- hard-boiled eggs, sliced in halves or quarters
- caper berries
- small tender leaves of romaine lettuce

Arrange ingredients attractively on a large tray or platter. Place the scoop of ricotta cheese in the center of the platter and garnish with parsley or curly lettuce.

Make-Your-Own Ice Cream Sundae Bar

Use your imagination and serve several varieties of ice cream with as many toppings as you wish:

- chocolate fudge sauce
- butterscotch sauce
- strawberry sauce
- sliced bananas
- liqueurs
- chocolate bits
- chopped nuts
- sprinkles (chocolate or pastel)
- whipped cream
- cherries

MEXICAN PARTY THEME

Flag Colors

- green
- white
- red

Party Occasions

- a trip to Mexico
- a birthday party or honoring a friend
- Cinco de Mayo (5th of May)
- Christmas party (using the red and green flag colors)
- any informal gathering

MENU SUGGESTIONS

Cocktails:
- Mexican beer
- tequila with quinine or soda water
- sangria
- margaritas

Appetizer:
- Mexican layered dip (see page 126)
- guacamole (see page 127)
- mini quesadillas
- taco tartlets (see page 136)
- bean dip Mexicana (see page 126)

Entrée:
- sour cream chicken enchiladas

Sorbet:
- orange tequila sorbet

Breads:
- warm tortillas

Salad:
- mixed greens with sliced avocado, pitted and sliced black olives, chopped red onions, cherry tomatoes, tortilla strips, black beans or red kidney beans and corn, tossed with an oil and vinegar dressing

Dessert:
- flan
- Mexican wedding cakes

RECOMMENDED RECIPES

Mini Quesadillas

Cover one half of a small flour tortilla with grated cheddar (or half cheddar and half Monterey jack) cheese. Spread with finely chopped green onions. Fold over and bake in a preheated 350° oven for about 5 minutes or until the cheese melts. Cut into wedges and serve hot.

Sour Cream Chicken Enchiladas

Ingredients:

> 3 10 ounce cans Cream of Chicken soup
> 1 pint sour cream
> 1 4 ounce can green chilies, diced
> 4 cups sharp cheddar cheese, grated
> 15 corn tortillas
> 1/2 cup vegetable oil
> 4 to 6 cooked chicken breasts, diced
> 1 small can black olives, pitted and chopped

Combine soup, sour cream and chilies and set aside. Heat oil and immerse tortillas just long enough to soften, then remove and drain. Spoon 2 to 3 tablespoons of soup mixture onto each tortilla and sprinkle them with 3 tablespoons of cheese. Add the diced chicken, dividing it equally among the tortillas. Roll up tortillas and place seam side down on a lightly greased oblong bake dish. Sprinkle with more cheese and bake in a preheated 325° oven for 30 minutes. Top with chopped olives and bake for an additional 15 minutes. Serves 6 to 8.

(Nancy Nashu)

Tortilla Strips (for salad)

Lightly brush one side of 6 inch diameter corn or flour tortillas with melted butter. You might wish to sprinkle lightly with a mixture of garlic salt, cumin and chili powder. Cut into thin strips and place on an ungreased baking sheet. Bake in a preheated 400° oven for 8 to 10 minutes or until crisp.

Orange Tequila Sorbet

Ingredients:

> 4 cups orange juice (about 10 medium oranges)
> 1 cup powdered sugar
> 1/2 cup tequila
> 1/2 cup lime juice (about 8 limes)

Mix orange juice and sugar together. Blend in tequila and lime juice. Place in ice cream maker and freeze. If you don't have an ice cream maker, place in a pan in the freezer until *just* frozen. Remove and break up with a fork until mushy, then return to the freezer. Serve in small individual ramekins or in orange or lime shells with the pulp removed. (To remove pulp, soak in hot water for 10 minutes. Invert and pull the pulp away from the skin). Makes 15 to 20 servings.

Flan (caramel custard)

Ingredients:

> 6 generous tablespoons sugar
> 4 eggs
> 3/4 cup sugar
> 1 12 ounce can evaporated milk
> 3/4 cup whole milk
> 1 teaspoon vanilla

Spread one generous tablespoon of sugar evenly over the bottoms of six 4 ounce ramekins or custard cups. Place in a preheated 350° oven and heat for 40 to 45 minutes or until the sugar has melted to a golden brown syrup. Remove from oven. Set aside to cool until the syrup has hardened, about 10 minutes. Beat the eggs. Stir in 3/4 cup sugar, evaporated milk, whole milk and vanilla. Stir well until sugar is dissolved. Pour into ramekins and place in a pan filled to about one inch with boiling water. Bake in a preheated 350° oven for about 45 minutes or until a knife inserted in the center of the custard comes out clean. Remove from oven and cool on a rack. Chill.

When ready to serve, run the tip of a knife around the sides of each ramekin and invert it into a shallow serving dish. Serve with a topping of whipped cream dusted with toasted, slivered almonds, or leave plain. Serves 6.

Should you prefer to make this flan in a single large dish, spread 1/2 cup sugar on the bottom of an 8 inch Pyrex or bake dish, and proceed as above. It may take a little longer, however, for the sugar to melt into syrup and the custard to bake.

Mexican Wedding Cakes (cookies)

Ingredients:

> 1 cup flour, sifted
> 1/2 cup (1 stick) butter, softened
> 2 tablespoons sugar
> pinch of salt
> 1 cup walnuts, finely ground
> 1/2 cup mini chocolate chips (optional)
> powdered sugar

Cream butter. Add sugar and mix thoroughly. Add flour, salt, vanilla, nuts, and if desired, mini chocolate chips and mix well. Roll into small balls about the size of a walnut and place on a lightly greased baking sheet. Bake in a preheated 400° oven for about 10 minutes or until lightly browned. Remove from oven, cool slightly.

Roll in powdered sugar. Colored sugar, available at specialty stores and some markets, can be added to the powdered sugar if desired. Makes about 2 1/2 dozen cookies.

IRISH PARTY THEME

Flag Colors

- Green
- White
- Orange

Party Occasions

- A trip to Ireland
- a birthday party or honoring a friend
- Saint Patrick's Day
- any informal gathering

MENU SUGGESTIONS

Appetizer:
- round of Brie cheese sprinkled with finely chopped parsley and chopped green onions, served with crackers
- spinach dip with crudities (see page 128) served in hollowed out green cabbage or green peppers

Entrée:
- Irish stew served in bread bowls or with green mashed potatoes

Salad:
- mixed greens with avocado, tossed with a green goddess dressing
- cole slaw

Desserts:
- lime sherbet with sugar cookie cutouts, with green icing
- lime (or lemon) curd tarts
- cheesecake with sliced kiwi fruit decoration

Beverage:
- Irish coffee

RECOMMENDED RECIPES

Irish Stew

Ingredients:

> 8 pounds lean lamb leg or rump, or lean beef, cut into 2 inch cubes
> flour
> 1 tablespoon salt
> 1/2 teaspoon pepper
> 6 to 8 tablespoons vegetable oil
> 4 onions, sliced
> 2 tablespoons sugar
> 6 cups dry red wine (or enough to cover 2/3 of the meat)
> 1 16 ounce can tomato purée
> 2 teaspoons dried basil
> 1 teaspoon dried thyme
> 4 teaspoons orange rind, grated
> 4 cloves garlic, crushed
> 2 pounds frozen baby carrots, thawed; or fresh, peeled and cut into 2 inch lengths, 1 inch wide
> 1 pound small fresh mushrooms

Dry meat thoroughly. Combine flour, salt and pepper and dredge meat in the mixture. Heat oil in a large heavy casserole or Dutch oven. Sauté meat in batches over moderately high heat until browned on all sides. After browning, remove meat and set aside. To same saucepan, add onions and sugar. Sauté, stirring constantly, until onions are glazed and slightly browned. Add a little more oil if pan becomes too dry. After onions are sautéed, pour off excess oil and add wine. Over moderate heat, stirring constantly, scrape up all residue which has accumulated on the bottom of the pan and cook for 2 minutes. Stir in tomato purée, basil, thyme, orange rind and garlic. Add browned meat, cover, and bring to a slow boil. Remove from heat and place in a

preheated 325° oven. Bake for 2 to 3 hours, stirring occasionally, until the meat is fork tender. If sauce bubbles rapidly, reduce oven temperature to 300°, so the juices will not evaporate. Remove from oven, and if not serving immediately, place a damp clean dish towel directly on top of the meat to prevent it from drying out. Stew may be refrigerated for up to 4 days, or frozen and held for longer periods.

Before serving, cook carrots in boiling water for 10 to 15 minutes or until almost tender. Drain. Remove all fat from surface of the stew. Add carrots and mushrooms and simmer on top of the stove at moderately high heat or return to a preheated 325° oven, stirring occasionally, for about 30 minutes or until heated thoroughly and the carrots are tender. Season to taste with additional wine, salt, pepper and grated orange rind. Serve in bread bowls (see below) or with green mashed potatoes. Serves 16.
(Marlene Sorosky, *Cooking for Holidays and Celebrations*)

Author's Note: This recipe can easily be cut in half.

Instructions for Irish stew bread bowls:

Hollow out six inch long French rolls, one per person to be served. Spread inside with garlic butter (see below) and place on the buffet next to the Irish stew so your guests can serve themselves.

Ingredients for garlic butter for bread bowls:

Combine and blend thoroughly 1 cup (2 sticks) of softened butter with 4 crushed garlic cloves and 4 tablespoons of minced parsley. Provides enough to spread 14 to 16 bread bowls.

Green Mashed Potatoes

Ingredients:

> 6 large potatoes
> 3/4 cup light cream
> 1/4 pound (1 stick) butter, at room temperature
> 2 teaspoons salt
> 1 teaspoon sugar
> 1/4 teaspoon white pepper
> 2 tablespoons chives, chopped
> 1 1/2 teaspoons dill
> 1 box frozen chopped spinach, thawed and most
>   moisture pressed out

Peel potatoes and boil until tender. Mash or put through a ricer. Beat in cream, butter, salt, sugar and pepper. Whip until fluffy. Stir in chives, dill and spinach. Mix thoroughly. Place in greased shallow 2 quart casserole dish. Bake in preheated 350° oven until piping hot, at least 30 minutes. Serves 8 to 10. (Nancy Nashu)

Cole Slaw

Ingredients:

> 1 cup mayonnaise
> 1/2 cup green onions, chopped
> 2 tablespoons red wine vinegar
> 1 tablespoon sweet pickle juice
> 1/2 teaspoon garlic salt
> 3/4 teaspoon caraway seeds
> 1/2 teaspoon salt
> 1/2 teaspoon pepper
> 4 cups cabbage, chopped

Mix together above ingredients and pour over cabbage. Mix well and refrigerate. Stir now and then before serving. Can be made the day before. Serves 6 to 8. (Nancy Nashu)

Lime (or Lemon) Curd Tarts

Ingredients for lime (or lemon) curd tart shells:

> 1 1/2 cups unsifted all purpose flour
> 1/3 cup powdered sugar
> 1/4 cup (1 stick) plus 1 tablespoon cold unsalted butter,
>   cut into pieces
> 1 whole egg
> 1 to 2 tablespoons ice water

Mix flour, sugar and butter in a food processor until mixture looks like coarse meal. Add egg. Mix, adding just enough water for dough to form into a ball (do not over mix or you will not have a flaky crust). If mixing by hand, mix flour and sugar in a mixing bowl and cut in butter with two knives until mixture looks like coarse meal. With a fork, mix in egg and just enough water to allow the dough to form into a ball.

Wrap in plastic wrap and refrigerate for several hours. Pinch off small walnut-sized pieces of dough with hands and press into tart shells or pans. Trim edges. Line each shell with wax paper or aluminum foil, and fill with beans, rice or pie weights. Bake in preheated 400° oven for about 10 minutes. Remove weights and wax paper or foil and continue baking for another 5 minutes, or until pastry is golden brown and flaky. Cool on wire racks. Carefully remove shells from tart pans. If the shells do not come out easily, freeze the pans and then remove the shells. These shells can be made ahead and frozen, either before or after baking. Makes 2 to 3 dozen one inch shells, fewer if larger tart pans are used.

Ingredients for lime curd tart filling:

> 1 1/3 cups sugar
> 1 3/4 sticks unsalted butter
> 2/3 cup lime juice
> 4 whole eggs
> 4 egg yolks
> 1 tablespoon grated lime peel

Place the ingredients in a non-aluminum double boiler or medium sized pan set over boiling water. Stir mixture constantly until it thickens, but do not let it boil. Transfer to non-aluminum refrigerator container and allow to cool.

When cool, add a drop of green food coloring, just enough to lightly color the mixture (if you get it too green it will not be very appetizing). Cover with plastic wrap and refrigerate until you are ready to fill the tarts, but do not keep the filling refrigerated for more than two weeks. Any filling left over or extra filled tarts can be frozen for future use.

After tarts have been filled, decorate with small sprigs of mint or a white chocolate candy leaf made from individual candy molds (see Catalog –Maid of Scandinavia, page 35).

Ingredients for lemon curd tart filling:

In the above recipe, substitute lemon juice for lime juice and grated lemon peel for grated lime peel, and omit the food coloring.

Irish Coffee

In each glass or cup, put 1 1/2 teaspoons sugar and dissolve in a small amount of hot coffee. Add 1 jigger (1 1/2 ounces) of Irish whiskey and fill to one inch of the top with hot coffee. Float 2 tablespoons of lightly whipped cream on top of each glass or cup. As an alternative to the whipped cream, spoon on heavy cream until it is about 1/2 inch deep. Sprinkle with freshly grated nutmeg (optional).

HAWAIIAN PARTY THEME

Flag Colors

- Red
- white
- blue

Party Occasions

- a trip to Hawaii
- a birthday party or honoring a friend
- a luau
- a garden/patio party
- a beach party
- any informal gathering

MENU SUGGESTIONS

Appetizers:
- marinated beef on a stick
- chutney kumaki Hana Maui
- shrimp with cocktail sauce or dip (see page 127)
- pineapple cheese ball

Entrée:
- barbecued beef (including spareribs) and/or chicken. Use your favorite sweet-and-sour sauce or barbecue sauce/marinade (if a weather change prevents an outdoor barbecue, bake this entrée in the oven)

Salad:
- mixed greens with chunks of fresh pineapple and avocado, tossed with Mauna Lau dressing, then sprinkled with chopped and toasted macadamia nuts

Bread/rolls:
- coconut muffins

Dessert:
- fresh papaya halves filled with coffee ice cream, flambée

RECOMMENDED RECIPES

Marinated Beef on a Stick

Ingredients:

> 1 finger fresh ginger root, about 3 inches
> 1 whole garlic bulb, separated and peeled
> 1 cup sugar
> 1/2 cup salad oil
> 1/4 cup soy sauce
> 1/4 cup sherry wine
> 1 to 1 1/2 pounds beef sirloin or beef tenderloin

Chop ginger root and garlic very fine, and place in a mixing bowl. Add sugar and mix well. Stir in salad oil, soy sauce and wine. Cut beef into very thin strips, cutting on the bias. Place in marinade. Beef sirloin needs to be marinated for at least two hours; beef tenderloin needs only one hour. Remove from marinade and skewer on bamboo sticks using 3 to 4 pieces of beef on each skewer. Place on barbecue and quickly turn from one side to the other, basting as they cook. Or you may broil them in the oven 3 to 4 inches from the flame for about 3 minutes on a side, basting as you turn them over. You will need about 18 to 20 skewers.   (Chef Rene Colin, Hana Maui Hotel)

Mauna Lau Dressing

Combine 1/2 cup cider vinegar, 1/4 cup pineapple juice, 3/4 teaspoon salt, 1 tablespoon sugar, dash of freshly ground pepper, 1/2 cup salad oil, 1/2 cup sesame oil and 1 teaspoon lemon juice. Shake well. Can be refrigerated for up to three weeks.
          (Roana and Gene Schindler, *Hawaiian Cookbook*)

Chutney Kumaki Hana Maui

Ingredients:

> 1 pound bacon, sliced
> 1 tablespoon prepared mustard
> 2 tablespoons brown sugar
> 1/4 cup Major Grey's (or homemade) chutney
> 1 8 ounce can water chestnuts, drained

Fry bacon until well done but still soft. Drain on paper towels. Spread mustard lightly on one side of each piece of bacon. Sprinkle evenly with brown sugar and set aside.

Remove fruit from chutney, chop very fine, and return to the chutney syrup. Dip each water chestnut into chutney and wrap with a piece of bacon with mustard-coated side up.

Secure the ends of the bacon with a wooden toothpick. Place bacon-wrapped water chestnuts on a baking pan and bake in a preheated 400° oven for 5 to 10 minutes, or until the bacon is crisp. Serve warm. Makes 14 to 16 servings.   (Chef Rene Colin, Hana Maui Hotel)

Pineapple Cheese Ball

Ingredients:

> 2 8 ounce packages cream cheese, softened
> 1 8 1/2 ounce can crushed pineapple, drained
> 2 cups pecans, chopped
> 1/4 cup green pepper, finely chopped
> 2 tablespoons onion, finely chopped
> 1 tablespoon seasoned salt
> canned pineapple slices
> maraschino cherries
> parsley sprigs

In a medium bowl, beat cream cheese with a fork until smooth. Gradually stir in crushed pineapple, 1 cup of pecans, the green pepper, onion and salt. Shape into a ball and roll in the remaining pecans. Wrap in plastic wrap and refrigerate until well chilled, at least overnight. Place cheese ball on a serving platter. Garnish with pineapple slices, cherries and parsley. Surround with crackers.

(Lucille Maxwell)

Coconut Muffins

Ingredients:

> 2 eggs
> 1/2 cup sugar
> 1/2 cup butter or margarine, melted
> 3/4 cup milk
> 2 teaspoons lemon rind, grated
> 1 1/2 cups sweetened coconut flakes
> 1 1/2 cups cake flour
> 1 1/2 teaspoons baking powder
> 1/2 teaspoon baking soda
> 1/4 teaspoon salt.

In a large bowl, combine eggs, sugar, butter, milk, lemon rind and coconut flakes. Mix well. In a smaller bowl, combine flour, baking powder, baking soda and salt. Mix well. Fold the dry mixture into the liquid mixture, stirring only enough to combine the two mixtures. Spoon into greased muffin pans and place in preheated 400° oven. (Fill any unused cups in the muffin pan with water to prevent the muffins or the pan from burning). Bake for 20 to 25 minutes, until golden brown on top and a cake tester comes out clean. Remove from pan and cool on a rack. Makes 14 medium muffins or 26 miniature muffins.

(Angela Clubb, *Wild About Muffins)*

Papaya-Coffee Ice Cream Flambée

For each guest, remove seeds from half a papaya and fill with coffee ice cream. Pour a small amount of Cointreau over the ice cream and put a dollop of whipped cream on top. Soak sugar cubes in lemon extract and place one cube on the top of each mound of whipped cream. Ignite just before serving.

(Chef Rene Colin, Hana Maui Hotel)

HOLLAND PARTY THEME

Flag Colors

- red
- white
- blue

Party Occasions

- a trip to Holland
- a birthday party or honoring a friend
- dinner by the fire
- fun for all ages.
- any informal gathering

MENU SUGGESTIONS

Appetizers:
- salted pecans and almonds (see page 129)
- popcorn mix
- pretzels
- carrots with dill (see page 130)
- zesty marinated carrots (see page 130)

Entrée:
- Dutch cheese fondue

Salad:
- mixed greens with tomato chunks, avocado chunks, crumbled crispy bacon, chopped green onions, tossed with your favorite oil and vinegar dressing
- fresh spinach leaves torn into pieces crumbled crispy bacon, chopped green onions, chopped hard-boiled eggs, tossed with your favorite oil and vinegar dressing

Dessert:
- orange fantasia
- vanilla ice cream topped with Grand Marnier and toasted slivered almonds
- lemon or lime sherbet balls topped with Cointreau
- brown sugar cookies (see page 148) to be served with any of the above

RECOMMENDED RECIPES

Popcorn Mix

To popped popcorn, add melted butter mixed with any or all of the following: freshly grated Parmesan cheese, garlic salt, mixed herbs (such as Mayacama Herb Mix, see Catalogs, page 34), and nuts (almonds, peanuts, cashews). You might prefer to serve the nuts separately and mix mini pretzels with the popcorn.

Dutch Cheese Fondue

You will need a fondue pot (or any flameproof enameled casserole or chafing dish) for each table. To keep the fondue smooth during dinner, encourage each guest to give the pot a good stir each time he or she dips bread cubes into it. Use denatured alcohol for the alcohol-burning pots and chafing dishes; otherwise, use votive candles or canned heat. Ingredients for each fondue pot:

Ingredients:

> 2 cups dry white wine or beer
> 1 medium garlic clove, peeled and slightly" bruised" with
>   the flat of a knife
> 1 pound Dutch Gouda cheese, coarsely grated, at room
>   temperature
> 1 tablespoon cornstarch
> 2 tablespoons Kirsch liqueur (too much makes the fondue
>   bitter)
> 1/8 teaspoon nutmeg
> 1/8 teaspoon salt
> 4 drops Worcestershire sauce or Tabasco sauce (optional)
> freshly ground pepper to taste
> 1 large loaf French or Italian bread, cut into 1 inch cubes,
>   including the crust

Pour the wine or beer into a 2 quart fondue pot. Drop in the garlic and bring to a boil over high heat, allowing to boil for 1 or 2 minutes. With a slotted spoon, remove the garlic and discard. Lower the heat so the liquid barely simmers. Stirring constantly with a table fork, add the cheese a handful at a time. Let each handful melt completely before adding another.

In a separate dish, mix the cornstarch and the Kirsch. Add this to the cheese mixture and stir until the fondue is creamy and smooth. Stir in nutmeg, salt and pepper to taste, and either the Worcestershire or Tabasco sauce if desired.

To serve, place the fondue pot over the heat in the center of the table, regulating the heat so the fondue mixture barely simmers. Place a basket of bread cubes nearby. Each guest spears a cube of bread onto a fondue fork (or skewer) and swirls the bread in the fondue until it is thoroughly coated. Eat immediately.

For variety, try wrapping a thin slice of cooked ham around the bread cubes before dipping them into the fondue. Each fondue pot will serve 4 to 6.   (SS Rotterdam, Holland American Line)

Orange Fantasia

Ingredients:

> 8 to 9 large navel oranges
> 2 cups sugar
> 1 cup water
> 1 tablespoon Grand Marnier
> 1 cup whipping cream
> 2 tablespoons powdered sugar
> 1/2 teaspoon vanilla
> 1/2 cup almonds, slivered and toasted

Using a peeler or stripper, remove peel from the oranges. Julienne (cut into slivers) the orange peel and set aside. From the orange, remove and discard the pith and separate the oranges into sections. Cut each section in half, transfer to a mixing bowl and set aside. In a small saucepan, over a low heat, combine the sugar and water, and stir until the sugar is dissolved. Let mixture boil for about 5 minutes without stirring.

Remove from heat and allow syrup to cool. Add Grand Marnier to the orange segments and toss lightly. Blend in 1/4 cup of syrup to coat the oranges evenly.

Lightly oil a baking sheet. Return the remaining syrup to a boil, add the julienned orange peel, and boil for 5 minutes. Remove the orange peel with a slotted spoon and spread on the prepared baking sheet to cool. Divide the orange segments evenly among your serving dishes. Combine the whipping cream, powdered sugar and vanilla, and whip until stiff. Top oranges with a generous dollop of whipped cream, and sprinkle with nuts and orange peel. Serves 10.

(Ann and Leonard Drabkin, *Bon Appétit*)

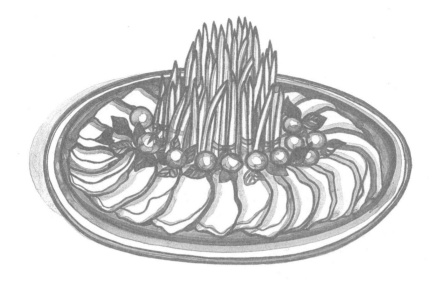

ENGLISH PARTY THEME

Flag Colors

- Red
- white
- blue

Party Occasions

- a trip to the United Kingdom
- a birthday party or honoring a friend
- a formal dinner
- an engagement or anniversary dinner
- any informal gathering

Note: These are all good occasions to get out your best china and crystal, and dine by candlelight

MENU SUGGESTIONS

Appetizers:
- salted pecans or salted almonds (see page 129)
- cheese crock with crackers (see page 136)

Entrée:
- roast beef or beef tenderloin with horseradish sauce and Yorkshire pudding (or popovers – use your favorite popover recipe)

Vegetable:
- *haricots verts* (small, slim green beans) with sliced almonds which have been sautéed in butter

Salad:
- mixed greens with avocado, mandarin oranges, crumbled bleu cheese, tossed with an oil and vinegar dressing
- hot curried fruit

Dessert:
- English trifle

RECOMMENDED RECIPES

Beef Tenderloin

Allow 1/2 pound of beef per person. If the meat is of uneven thickness, tuck the narrow end under to make it even. Brush with butter or oil and insert a meat thermometer. Roast in a preheated 450° oven for 10 to 12 minutes per pound of meat for rare; longer for more well done. (The meat thermometer will register about 120° for rare, 130° for medium rare, and 140° for well done).

Ingredients for horseradish sauce:

> 2 tablespoons sugar
> 1 egg, well beaten
> 2 tablespoons vinegar
> salt to taste
> 1/2 cup bottled horseradish
> 1 cup whipping cream, whipped

In a small pan, combine sugar, egg, vinegar and salt and cook until thick. Cool. Whip cream until stiff and fold into the above mixture along with the horseradish. Serves 6.

Ingredients for Yorkshire pudding:

> 2 cups flour, sifted
> 1/2 teaspoon salt
> 4 eggs, at room temperature
> 2 cups whole milk, at room temperature
> 1/2 cup (1 stick) butter, melted

Sift together the presifted flour and salt into a bowl. Separately beat together the eggs and milk, then stir into the flour mixture. Beat until well blended and large bubbles rise to the surface. Cover with plastic wrap and refrigerate for at least two hours, or overnight. Bring to room

temperature and beat again. About 1/2 hour before the roast is done, pour melted butter into a hot, ovenproof 9 inch by 13 inch dish, and set in a preheated 450° oven until sizzling hot. Remove from oven and pour in batter. Return to oven and bake for 20 minutes. Reduce heat to 350° and bake for about another 10 to 15 minutes or until puffed and golden brown. If you need more oven room, the roast may be removed from the oven and covered while baking the Yorkshire pudding. Cut into squares and serve while hot. Makes about 6 servings.

Hot Curried Fruit

Ingredients:

> 1 1 pound can each of peach, pear, and apricot halves
> 1 1 pound can of pineapple wedges (you can substitute
>   pineapple chunks or slices for the wedges)
> 1 small jar maraschino cherries
> 2 tablespoons margarine, at room temperature
> 2 tablespoons brown sugar
> 1 teaspoon curry powder
> 2 teaspoons cornstarch
> 1/2 teaspoon lemon rind, grated

Drain all fruit and place in 1 1/2 quart casserole. Mix gently. Blend together margarine, sugar, curry powder, cornstarch and lemon rind. Sprinkle over fruit. Let stand for several hours to draw out juice from the fruit. Place uncovered in a preheated 325° oven and bake for 1 hour, basting occasionally. Serve while hot. Serves 6.

English Trifle

Split ladyfingers, either homemade (see below) or purchased from the market, and line around the sides of a trifle bowl or deep glass serving bowl. Place a few on top of others on the bottom to make a partial double layer. Spread with raspberry jam. Sprinkle with sherry. (It may be easier to put the jam and sherry on the ladyfingers before arranging them in the bowl). Pour pudding sauce (see below) over all. Sprinkle with toasted, slivered almonds. Serves 6.

(Stuffed Shirt Restaurant, Pasadena)

Ingredients for English trifle ladyfingers:

> 4 eggs, separated
> 1/3 cup sugar
> 1/2 teaspoon lemon extract
> 3/4 cup flour, sifted

Butter and flour ladyfinger pan. Beat egg whites until stiff and set aside. Beat egg yolks and sugar until light in color and mixture forms a ribbon. Stir in lemon extract and flour. Blend in egg whites, mixing lightly. Spoon mixture into prepared pan using heaping teaspoons to make each ladyfinger. Place in preheated 375° oven and bake for 7 to 9 minutes, or until firm to the touch and lightly browned at the edges. Cool slightly and remove from the pan. Cool completely on wire rack. Sprinkle lightly with powdered sugar if desired. Makes about 36 ladyfingers, more than you will need for this trifle recipe. Any extra can be frozen for future use.

Ingredients for English trifle pudding sauce:

> 2 eggs, separated
> 1 cup powdered sugar
> 2 tablespoons sherry wine
> 1 cup whipping cream

Thoroughly beat egg yolks. Mix in powdered sugar. Add sherry and stir. Whip the whipping cream until stiff and fold into mixture. Beat egg whites until stiff and fold them into the mixture.

INDEX

Notes:

_____
_____
_____
_____
_____
_____
_____
_____
_____
_____
_____
_____
_____
_____
_____
_____
_____
_____
_____
_____
_____
_____
_____
_____
_____
_____
_____
_____